TERMS IN SYSTEMIC LINGUISTICS
A GUIDE TO HALLIDAY

Terms in Systemic Linguistics

A Guide to Halliday

Alex de Joia
and
Adrian Stenton

ST. MARTIN'S PRESS
NEW YORK

© Alex de Joia and Adrian Stenton 1980

All rights reserved. For information write:
St. Martin's Press, Inc., 175 Fifth Avenue, New York, NY 10010
Printed in Great Britain
First published in the United States of America in 1980

Library of Congress Catalog Number 80-5089

ISBN 0-312-79180-1

Contents

Foreword

It seemed to me that a Foreword to this book should serve two purposes. The first is to introduce the book; and I can do this very briefly by expressing appreciation to the editors, Alex de Joia and Adrian Stenton, for the admirable job they have done. They have thoroughly sifted through a large quantity of my written work and extracted from it those passages which they consider crucial to the understanding of key terms. By bringing together related material from widely scattered sources they have made it accessible and easy to follow.

The second purpose is to explain why it was they decided to undertake this project. I have no intention of anticipating what they have to say in their preface; but I should like to comment on the problem of terminology from my own point of view, in relation to the passages they have selected for inclusion. This may help to clarify the reasoning behind some of the concepts I used, and the labels I chose to assign to them.

It has always been my view that what was needed in linguistics was not so much new theories as new descriptions. Grammars in the received tradition were idealized, partial and limited in delicacy; they reflected their origins in the search for answers to questions that had been formulated many generations ago. This was not to belittle the work of the earlier grammarians; it goes without saying that anything one might achieve would be achieved by standing on the shoulders of the past. But the descriptive apparatus of traditional grammars could no longer be simply taken for granted; it needed not only extending but also reinterpreting and to a certain extent revising in the light of more recent knowledge. Now the prevailing trend in linguistics in the third quarter of this century was the opposite one to this: it was to accept traditional descriptions and adapt them to new theoretical constructs. In this my approach was out of line.

There is of course no very clear boundary between theory and description. Describing a language is a work of interpretation; and interpretation is a theoretical pursuit. New descriptions, therefore, enforce new theories. But this, as I see it, is where the theory comes from. I am not really a theoretician; I have been interested in theoretical matters only because I had to be, because it was necessary to construct some new theoretical framework in order to accommodate certain aspects of the interpretation I wanted to suggest. But the resources of language are extraordinarily rich, and the ways in which things can be related to each other are of an intricacy that we have hardly yet begun to conceive of. The theory should not restrict the kinds of interpretative statement we can make; it needs to be rich enough to allow for all kinds of elaborations and extensions— especially extensions in delicacy, given that what we know about language today is only a fragment of what there is to be found out— without having to be patched up and mended all the time. For this reason my conceptual apparatus has always been extravagant rather than parsimonious. Since I was drawing no conclusions from the form of the theory, beyond the obvious one that language must be such-and-such if such-and-such a theory can account for it, there was no virtue in restricting its scope.

This last point is related to the kinds of questions one is asking. For me language has always been object, not instrument. That is to say, my questions have been questions about language itself; I have not been using language as an instrument for asking questions about other things (though I have often used other things as instruments for asking questions about language). To take something as object means that you cannot ignore its complexity; you have to try and keep all of it in focus at once. Language is a complex object, comprising both system and process—the language, and the text. A description of text is one-sided if text is not being related to the linguistic system from which it is derived; equally, a description of the system is one-sided if the system is not shown to be the source that text is derived from. It is this perspective that has determined the directions my work has taken.

Finally, however much we may try to overview the linguistic system as a whole, there is an inherent directionality in its interpretation, which has consequences for the terminology. Linguistics evolved as a search for the meanings of forms: 'these are the forms; now this is what they mean'—although the terms used to label the forms were inevitably, for the most part, semantic ones, like singular, active, or transitive. But for some purposes it is useful to start from the other end: 'these are the meanings; now this is how they are expressed'. As a consequence, either the same terms have to be redefined as labels for the semantic patterns underlying these forms (with which however they are not in exact correspondence), or another set of terms has to be created. Neither solution seems particularly satisfactory.

The citations that have been assembled by the editors in this volume cover terms which fall mainly into a few general categories that may be identified within the perspective I have outlined. Because of my concern with the system, the basis of the description had to be paradigmatic; hence the need for names of *systems* (in Firth's sense) and of *features*, which are the terms in these systems. Because of my concern with the text, the elements of structure had to be *functional*, interpreting the role a given element was playing in the configuration of which it was a part. Most of the descriptive terms are of one or other of these three kinds; and because of the orientation, from meanings to forms, they had to represent 'facts' of semantics rather than 'facts' of grammar. Then there are a few terms that were required for general theoretical purposes, especially concerning the functional organization of the linguistic system and the relation of text to context of situation. To show what I mean, let me give one or two examples of problems that arose under each of these headings.

Systems. Some grammatical systems have long-established names, like *number* and *voice*; but there are some surprising gaps. When I was writing my Ph.D. thesis in the early fifties I could find no name for the system 'non-negative/negative'; so I called it *polarity*. The system defined by 'indicative (declarative/interrogative) / imperative' I referred to as *mood*, distinguishing this from *modality* meaning the system(s) expressed by (among other things) modal auxiliaries. For the system determining the number and kinds of participant in the clause it seemed natural to generalize the term *transitivity*, by extension from transitive/intransitive as labels for the syntactic potential of the verb. Other systems which needed names were *theme* (*thematization* would have been better, though more cumbersome), *information* (for the distribution of given and new), *key* (for the subcategories of mood realized in English by tone) and *finiteness*.

Features (terms in systems). There was no term for 'not negative' in the polarity system (the overlapping concept of 'affirmative' was at once too broad and too narrow); so it seemed natural to call it *positive*. This left *affirmative* free to mean 'not interrogative', and I used it in this sense in my early writings until it was overtaken by *declarative*, which I then adopted. The most difficult area was that of transitivity. How does one label the semantic systems that lie behind transitive and intransitive, active and passive, and the like? For (semantic) 'voice' in Chinese, in the fifties, I had used *active, passive* and *ergative*. Writing of English in the early sixties I tried *operative* and *receptive* for 'voice'; and *extensive* (*effective/descriptive*) / *intensive* for 'transitivity'—types of process distinguished by their participant structures. The latter I subsequently replaced with a set of more meaningful terms referring directly to the types of process themselves: *materials, mental, verbal* and *relational*.

Functions. As a student of Firth's I was brought up to be shy of functional labels; but for various reasons I came to need them, and from the late fifties have used terms such as *Subject, Actor, Theme, Complement* and so on (always with an initial capital as signature). There were many gaps in this terminology; for example, it was necessary to supply even such basic terms as *Beneficiary* (for 'logical indirect object') and *Range* (for 'logical cognate object'). Perhaps the most serious gap—but this was a conceptual gap, not merely a terminological one—was that function in an ergative construction which corresponds to the Goal in a non-middle ('transitive') and Actor in a middle ('intransitive'): the element through which the process is actualized. This is a function which is clearly defined in the grammar of English. In 1965 I started calling it the *Affected*, and it appears under this name in a number of papers; early in the seventies I altered this to *Medium*, but very little of what I have done in this area since that time has been published, so the term is recognized only by those who have heard me talk on the subject.

Of the more important theoretical terms, *system* and *structure* come from Firth. I introduced *rank* to refer to a constituent hierarchy based on functional units—and hence closely related to the folk-linguistic model—in contradistinction to the formal 'immediate constituent' type; and from rank came *rank shift*, which I never liked but could think of no alternative to. When *embedding* was introduced I would have liked to go over to it, but could not because the two were not synonymous: embedding conflates the concepts of rank shift and hypotaxis, whereas it has always seemed to me necessary to make a clear theoretical distinction between these two—hypotaxis as a dependency relation in the system, rank shift as a structural mechanism whereby an element comes to occupy a function in a structure of its own or some lower rank. One of the most pervasive concepts is that of *delicacy*, the characterization of a system by progressive discrimination—a sort of paradigmatic analogue of constituent hierarchy; the term was suggested by Angus McIntosh in 1959. For the functional components of the semantic system, *ideational, interpersonal* and *textual*, the alternatives that I was aware of were based on such different conceptions of 'function' in language that it seemed better to use a distinct set which corresponded more closely to what I meant.

Wherever possible I have followed established practice, neither creating new terms nor redefining old ones. Despite what the appearance of a book such as this might suggest, the majority of technical expressions in my writings are ordinary linguistic terms used in ordinary ways. But like any other linguistic item, a technical term derives its meaning from its environment, the paradigmatic and syntagmatic contexts in which it is used. What counts is the total lexico-semantic ecological system. In order to be understood, one tries to use terms consistently and in such a way that they fit together into a coherent schema. Needless to say, the intention is not always matched by achievement; for one thing, the schema itself is likely to evolve and change through time. The editors have built in the diachronic dimension by presenting the terms in different environments representing different stages. In this way they have made things intelligible without making it seem that they have always fitted into a fixed mosaic of conceptual design.

M. A. K. Halliday

Acknowledgements

The authors and publisher of this book wish to thank the following for permission to quote from the previously published works of M. A. K. Halliday: M. A. K. Halliday, *Educational Review*, Edward Arnold, *Foundations of Language*, Georgetown University, *Journal of Linguistics, Linguistics, Lingua*, Longmans, John Lyons, Mouton, The Philological Society, Rand Corporation, University College (London), and *Word*.

Preface

The year 1976 marked two decades in the publishing life of Michael Halliday. And those twenty years saw a number of important changes. He moved from the strict formalism of 'Categories of the Theory of Grammar,' through the abstraction of 'Some Notes on Deep Grammar' to the social outlook of *Language and Social Man*. But there was a great deal of stability too, for example in the central position given to explanation in terms of function.

We felt that it was an appropriate time to stop and chart both the changes and the constants, and this book is the result.

It is a collection of citations from Halliday's work during this period. The citations are grouped thematically and chronologically, and supplemented and cross-referenced by an extensive 'Alphabetical Listing of Terms'. We hope that the book will prove to be useful in two ways. Its thematic arrangement means that if you want to get a general idea of what Halliday means by 'function', you can simply turn to Chapter 3 and browse through it. To this end each citation is intended to be able to stand on its own. If you want to put 'function' in a broader, or narrower, perspective, to explore more thoroughly its relationship to other terms, and to other parts of the theory, you can then work from the Alphabetical Listing backwards, and you will be directed to all those citations, in whatever chapter, which are specifically relevant. The Alphabetical Listing is thus a much more complete and accurate list than the contents alone.

Each citation has another context, of course, and this is the work from which it was drawn. Indeed, one of the broader aims of this book is to direct the reader to the appropriate paper or book by Halliday, to put it in the larger context of Halliday's work as a whole, to tie it in with earlier and with subsequent writings, a function served by the chronological listing of citations under each heading.

Alex de Joia & Adrian J. Stenton
Hatfield

Bibliography

Books and Articles by M. A. K. Halliday

In this list the date preceding each entry is the one that has been used to locate the citation. As far as possible this is the date of first publication. Where two dates appear for one entry, e.g. 1961/66, the article has been revised, and we are citing the revised version. The remainder of the reference is the most easily available location of the article.

1956a 'Grammatical categories in Modern Chinese' *Transactions of the Philological Society* 1956. 177–224. (Extract in Kress, G. R. 1976. 36–51.)

1956b 'The linguistic basis of a mechanical thesaurus' *Mechanical Translation* 1956 3.3. 81–8.

1957 'Some aspects of systematic description and comparison in grammatical analysis' in Firth, J. R. 1957. 54–67.

1959 *The Language of the Chinese 'Secret History of the Mongols'* Oxford: Blackwell 1959.

1961 'Categories of the theory of grammar' *Word* 1961 17.3. 241–92. (Extract in Kress, G. R. 1976. 52–72.)

1961/66 'General linguistics and its application to language teaching' in McIntosh, A. and Halliday, M. A. K. 1966. 1–41

1962/66 'Linguistics and machine translation' in McIntosh, A. and Halliday, M. A. K. 1966. 145–58.

1963a 'Class in relation to the axes of chain and choice in language' *Linguistics* 1963 2. 5–15. (Extract in Kress, G. R. 1976. 84–7.)

1963b 'The tones of English' *Archivum Linguisticum* 1963 15.1. 1–28.

1963c 'Intonation in English grammar' *Transactions of the Philological Society* 1963. 143–69.

1964a 'Descriptive linguistics in literary studies' in McIntosh, A. and Halliday, M. A. K. 1966. 56–69.

1964b *The Linguistic Sciences and Language Teaching* London: Longman 1964. (With McIntosh, A. and Strevens, P.)

1964c 'Syntax and the consumer' in O'Brien, R. 1968. 189–202.

1964/67 'The linguistic study of literary texts' in Chatman, S. and Levin, S. R. 1967. 217–23.

1964/76 'English system networks' in Kress, G. R. 1976. 101–35.

1966a 'Some notes on "deep" grammar' *Journal of Linguistics* 1966 2.1. 57–67. (Extract in Kress, G. R. 1976. 88–98.)

1966b 'The concept of rank: a reply' *Journal of Linguistics* 1966 2.1. 110–18.

1966c 'Lexis as a linguistic level' in Bazell, C. E. et al. 1966. 148–62. (Extract in Kress, G. R. 1976. 73–83.)

1966d 'Typology and the exotic' in McIntosh, A. and Halliday, M. A. K. 1966. 165–82.

1966e 'Intonation systems in English' in McIntosh, A. and Halliday, M. A. K. 1966. 111–33.

1966/76 'The English verbal group' in Kress, G. R. 1976. 136–58.

1967a 'Linguistics and the teaching of English' in Britton, J. 1967. 80–90.

1967b 'Notes on transitivity and theme in English, Part 1' *Journal of Linguistics* 1967 3.1. 37–81.

1967c 'Notes on transitivity and theme in English, Part 2' *Journal of Linguistics* 1967 3.2. 199–244.

1967d *Some Aspects of the Thematic Organization of the English Clause* Santa Monica: The Rand Corporation 1967 (Extract in Kress, G. R. 1976. 174–88.)

1967e *Intonation and Grammar in British English* The Hague: Mouton 1967.

1967f *Grammar, Society and the Noun* London: H. K. Lewis 1967.

1968a 'Notes on transitivity and theme in English, Part 3' *Journal of Linguistics* 1968 4.2. 179–215.

1968b 'Language and experience' *Educational Review* 1968 20.2. 95–106.

1969a 'Options and functions in the English clause' in Householder, F. W. 1972. 248–57.

1969b 'Relevant models of language' in Halliday, M. A. K. 1973c. 9–21.

1969/76a 'Systemic grammar' in Kress, G. R. 1976. 3–6.

1969/76b 'Types of process' in Kress, G. R. 1976. 159–73.

1970a *A Course in Spoken English: Intonation* London: Oxford University Press 1970. (Extract in Kress, G. R. 1976. 214–34.)

1970b 'Language structure and language function' in Lyons, J. 1970. 140–65.

1970c 'Functional diversity in language as seen from a consideration of modality and mood in English' *Foundations of Language* 1970 6.3. 322–61. (Extract in Kress, G. R. 1976. 189–213.)

1971a 'Language in a social perspective' in Halliday, M. A. K. 1973c. 48–71.

1971b 'A "linguistic approach" to the teaching of the mother tongue?' *The English Quarterly* 1971 4.2 13–24.

1971c 'Language acquisition and initial literacy' in Douglass, M. P. 1971. 63–8.

1971d 'Linguistic function and literary style: an enquiry into the language of William Golding's *The Inheritors*' in Halliday, M. A. K. 1973c. 103–43.

1972a 'Towards a sociological semantics' in Halliday, M. A. K. 1973c. 72–102.

1972b 'National language and language planning in a multilingual society' *East African Journal* 1972 November.

1973a 'The functional basis of language' in Halliday, M. A. K. 1973c. 22–47. (Extract in Kress, G. R. 1976. 7–25.)

1973b Foreword in Bernstein, B. 1973. ix-xvi.

1973c *Explorations in the Functions of Language* London: Edward Arnold 1973.

1973d Foreword in Mackay, D. et al. 1973. iii-x.

1973e Introduction in Halliday, M. A. K. 1973c. 7, 8.

1974a *Lanuage and Social Man* London: Longman 1974.

1974b Discussion in Parret, H. 1974. 81–120.

1974c 'The place of "functional sentence perspective" in the system of linguistic description' in Danes, F. 1974. 43–53. (Extract in Kress, G. R. 1976. 26–31.)

1975a 'Language as social semiotic: towards a general sociolinguistic theory' in Makkai, A. and Makkai, V. 1975. 17–46.

1975b 'Sociological aspects of semantic change' in Heilmann, L. 1975. 853–79.

1975c *Learning How to Mean—Explorations in the Development of Language* London: Edward Arnold 1975.

1976a '"The teacher taught the student English": an essay in applied linguistics' in Reich, P. A. 1976. 344–9.

1976b *Cohesion in English* London: Longman 1976. (With Hasan, R.)

Other books

BAZELL, C. E., CATFORD, J. C., HALLIDAY, M. A. K., and ROBINS, R. H. (eds) *In Memory of J. R. Firth* London: Longman 1966.

BERNSTEIN, BASIL (ed.) *Class, Codes and Control II: Applied Studies Towards a Sociology of Language* London: Routledge & Kegan Paul 1973.

BRITTON, JAMES (ed.) *Talking and Writing: A Handbook for English Teachers* London: Methuen 1967.

CHATMAN, SEYMOUR and LEVIN, SAMUEL R. (eds) *Essays on the Language of Literature* Boston: Houghton Mifflin 1967.

DANEŠ, FRANTIŠEK (ed.) *Papers on Functional Sentence Perspective* Prague: Academia 1974.

DOUGLASS, MALCOLM P. (ed.) *Claremont Reading Conference 35th Yearbook* 1971.

FIRTH, J. R. (ed.) *Studies in Linguistic Analysis* Oxford: Blackwell 1957.

HEILMANN, LUIGI (ed.) *Proceedings of the Eleventh International Congress of Linguists* Bologna: Il Mulino 1975.

HOUSEHOLDER, F. W. (ed.) *Syntactic Theory I Structuralist*. Harmondsworth Penguin 1972.

KRESS, GUNTHER R. (ed.) *Halliday: System and Function in Language* London: Oxford University Press 1976.

LYONS, JOHN (ed.) *New Horizons in Linguistics* Harmondsworth: Penguin Books 1970.

MACKAY, DAVID, THOMPSON, BRIAN, and SCHAUB, PAMELA *Breakthrough to Literacy: Teachers Resource Book* Glendale, California: Bowman 1973.

MAKKAI, ADAM and MAKKAI, VALERIE BECKER (eds) *The First LACUS Forum* Columbia, South Carolina: Hornbeam Press 1975.

MCINTOSH, ANGUS and HALLIDAY, M. A. K. *Patterns of Language:*

Papers in General, Descriptive and Applied Linguistics London: Longman 1966.

O'BRIEN, RICHARD J. (compiler) *Georgetown University Round Table Selected Papers in Linguistics 1961–1965* Washington, D.C.: Georgetown University Press 1968.

PARRET, HERMAN *Discussing Language* The Hague: Mouton 1974.

REICH, PETER A. (ed.) *The Second LACUS Forum* Columbia, South Carolina: Hornbeam Press 1976.

Notation

The citations are as originally published except for:

. . . (3 dots) word or words omitted

/ / (slant brackets) compilers' interpolation

Each citation is followed by the date of the source and its page reference (see Bibliography for full details).

1
Categories

1   ... the clause has a number of different but simultaneous constituent structures according to which set of options is being considered ... This explains the minimal bracketing: such a componential analysis of structural function presupposes a 'rank' (string constituent) rather than an 'immediate constituent' view of linguistic structure. (1969a, 255, 256)

2   ... any bracketing more than the necessary minimum is redundant, because the information it contains is recoverable from the systemic part of the description ... (1969/76a, 4)

3   ... two principal types of bracketing have been used in linguistics, which we might refer to as 'maximum bracketing' and 'minimum bracketing'. The former is what is known as 'immediate constituent' analysis, the latter has been called 'string constituent' analysis and is often associated with the 'slot and filler' account of structure. (1969/76a, 4)

4   In a systemic description the bracketing is minimal ... (1969/76a, 4)

5   ... non-minimal bracketing tends to be self-contradictory. (1969/76a, 5)

6   ... any item may have not just one structure but many. Since

1

there may be a number of simultaneous structures superimposed on one another in this way, minimal bracketing is the most neutral . . . (1969/76a, 5)

1.2 Categories

---

7 The grammatical categories to be established in the description are of three types: units, elements and classes. (1956a, 180)

8 The description of a language employs, at the grammatical level as at all other levels, systems of related categories. (1957, 54)

9 . . . there can be no universal formal-linguistic categories (there might theoretically be categories formally identified as common to all languages studied heretofore, but such identification is not yet a practical possibility), while non-formal-linguistic categories, if they are to figure in the description at all, must be implicitly regarded as universal. (1957, 54)

10 Even if any one category can be identified (presumably con-textually) across all language studies so far . . . such a category is universal only in the limited range of what is and has been, not what might be. (1957, 57)

11 At present any universal system of categories must rest on other than formal linguistic criteria: if such can be provided, for example, by mathematics, so much the better—the 'structural' linguist will not 'reject' it, but he cannot be expected to provide it within his own terms of reference. (1957, 57)

12 A complete analysis at the grammatical level, in a particular description in which all forms of the language are related to systems set up within the language itself, requires the establish-ment of grammatical categories, ordered as terms in interrelated systems and having as exponents the substantial (phonic or graphic) segments of the text. (1957, 58)

13 Such /grammatical/ categories are of two types, which we may call 'units' and 'classes'. (1957, 58)

14 The relevant theory consists of a scheme of interrelated categories which are set up to account for the data, and a set of scales of abstraction which relate the categories to the data and to each other. (1961, 243)

15 The fundamental categories for the theory are four: 'unit', 'structure', 'class' and 'system'. (1961, 247)

16 Each of the four /categories/ is specifically related to, and logically derivable from, each of the others. There is no relation of precedence or logical priority among them. They are mutually defining: as with theoretical categories in general, 'definition' in the lexicographical sense is impossible, since no one category is defined until all the others are, in the totality of the theory. (1961, 248)

17 The relation of these categories to each other and to the data involve three distinct scales of abstraction, those of 'rank', 'exponence', and 'delicacy' . . . (1961, 248)

18 As the primary categories of the theory, /unit, structure, class and system/ make possible a coherent account of what grammar is and of its place in language . . . (1961, 248)

19 If one asks, 'why these four /categories/, and not three, or five, or another four?', the answer must be: because language is like that—because these four, and no others, are needed to account for the data: that is, to account for all grammatical patterns that emerge by generalization from the data. (1961, 248)

20 . . . each category can be linked *directly* by exponence to the formal item: it is in fact a requirement of the theory that any descriptive category should be able to be so linked. (1961, 271)

21 . . . no relation whatever is presupposed between the categories required to state the distinction in form (grammar or lexis) and the *categories* required to state phonologically the distinction in substance which carries it. (1961, 283)

22 /the/ . . . categories—provide the framework for the grammatical description. They are bound up with the general linguistic theory. They are established as primitive categories of the theory and retained because they enable us to give a fairly simple account of all the facts, as simple as we could expect considering that we are dealing with such complex material as language. (1961/66, 15)

23 /Class, system, unit and structure/ are the four theoretical categories that are required if we want to account fully for the kind of patterning in language that we recognize as the level of grammar. (1964b, 24–5)

24 The *descriptive* categories, those used to talk about the grammar of any particular language, which . . . are instances of these theoretical categories /unit, structure, system and class/, are *not* universal and cannot be assumed to be found in all languages. Indeed, they must be redefined for each language. (1964b, 31)

25 With these four basic categories of unit, structure, system and class it is possible to describe the grammar of all languages. What is significant here is that in order to find anything 'universal' in grammar—common, that is, to the grammar of all languages—we have to go to the very high level of abstraction represented by these categories. Only such *theoretical* categories can be treated as universal. (1964b, 31)

26 One way of handling grammatical relations on these two axes /syntagmatic and paradigmatic/ is by reference to the theoretical categories of 'structure' and 'system', with the 'class' definable as that which enters into the relations so defined. In lexis these concepts need to be modified, and distinct categories are needed for which therefore different terms are desirable. (1966c, 152)

1.3 Chain

---

27 . . . I have used here the terms 'chain axis' and 'choice axis' in place of their less self-explanatory technical equivalents 'systematic axis' and 'paradigmatic axis'. (1963a, 5n)

28 The chain relations are 'structure', in grammar, and 'collocation' in lexis. (1964b, 35)

1.4 Class

29 The classes are systemic and are stated as paradigms in inter-relation with the elements; that is, as exhaustive inventories of forms classified as operating at a given place in the structure of the unit next above. (1956a, 181)

30 A class is said to be primary when it is the unique term operating at a particular place in structure. (1956a, 181)

31 . . . mutually independent systems of classes of any unit are referred to as 'dimensions': thus one dimension of clause-classes might be the 'aspect' dimension, with a system, say, of two terms, 'perfective' and 'imperfective'. (1957, 59)

32 There may be any number of dimensions of classes for each unit, but each dimension will by itself form an exhaustive system of classification such that every exponent of a given unit may be placed within it . . . (1957, 59)

33 . . . classes are set up independently of structures: that is to say, a unit . . . having been established, it is then classified by reference to various sets of formal criteria . . .; each set of criteria permits the establishment of one system of classes . . . (1957, 59)

34 Class, like structure, is variable in delicacy. (1961, 260)

35 The class is that grouping of members of a given unit which is defined by operation in the structure of the unit next above. It accounts for a 'paradigmatic' relation, being a grouping of items 'at risk' under certain conditions. It is related primarily to elements of structure: the first degree of classification yields classes which stand in one/one relation to elements of primary structures, and these we may call 'primary classes'. (1961, 260)

36 . . . the class–structure relation is constant—a class is always defined with reference to the structure of the unit next above, and the structure with reference to classes of the unit next below. (1961, 261)

37 Class, like structure, is linked to unit: a class is always a class of (members of) a given unit . . . (1961, 261)

38 A class is *not* a grouping of members of a given unit *which are alike in their own structure*. (1961, 261)

39 . . . by reference to the rank scale, *classes* are derived 'from above' (or 'downwards') and not 'from below' (or 'upwards'). (1961, 261)

40 When a name is needed for morphological groupings, . . . the term 'paradigm' is available. (1961, 262)

41 The class is a grouping of items identified by operation in structure, that is, what enters into grammatical relations of structure is not the item itself considered as a formal realization but the class, which is not *a list of* formal items but *an abstraction from* them. (1961, 264)

42 The class . . . is a grouping of the members of a given unit that have the same potentiality of occurrence. Moreover, each class is assignable to one unit: different units may have different classes. The class is that set of items which operate in the same way, playing the same role in the structure of the unit next above. There will of course be classes and sub-classes and sub-sub-classes, each more delicately differentiated according as one takes into account more and more delicate distinctions of structure. (1961/66, 12)

43 The class . . . is determined according to function in the structure of the unit above, that is, the unit immediately above. The relation is thus one of *downward* determination: it is the unit above that provides the basis for classes of the unit below. Upward analysis, giving groupings derived from below (that is, set of

6

items alike in their own structure), does not by itself produce classes—not, that is, unless the two groupings coincide.

There are of course many cases where the criteria of downward analysis and those of upward analysis do agree: so much the better. But when they do not, as is frequently the case, it is the criterion of downward analysis that is decisive. (1961/66, 12–13)

44 . . . 'paradigm' being the name of the grouping determined by upward analysis . . . (1961/66, 13)

45 It seems reasonable to use 'syntax' to refer to downward analysis, from sentence down to morpheme, and 'morphology' for upward analysis, from morpheme to sentence. Hence, one could say: the class is determined by syntactical and not by morphological considerations; in a word, classes are syntactical. (1961/66, 14)

46 I have assumed . . . that this category of *class* is to be defined syntactically. By this I mean that the concept is introduced into the description of a language in order to bring together those sets of items that have the same potentiality of occurrence; in other words, sets of items which are alike in the way they pattern in the structure of items of higher rank. (1963a, 5)

47 This use of the term 'class', to name a category defined in some way by its relationship to a higher structure, is by no means universal in linguistics; but it would probably be granted that some such category is necessary to linguistic description whatever name we choose to adopt for it. (1963a, 5)

48 It seems to me appropriate that the term 'class' should be reserved for the syntactic set (the morphological set may then be referred to as a 'type') . . . (1963a, 6–7)

49 It is also true, in my opinion, that the *class* thus defined, the syntactic set, is crucial to the whole of linguistic theory, since it is required to give meaning to the basic concept of 'structure' and 'system'; whereas the *type*, or morphological set, is more a descriptive convenience whose theoretical implications are largely internal to itself. (1963a, 7)

50 It is the class that enters into relations of structure and of system in language. (1963a, 7)

51 It is useful to be able to distinguish classes derived in these two ways: they can be referred to respectively as 'chain classes' (those relating to structure) and 'choice classes' (those relating to system). (1963a, 7)

52 It may be noted in passing that the one-member class has particular significance in linguistic theory: if grammar is taken to be that part of linguistic form in which choices are 'closed', by contrast with lexis (vocabulary) in which they are 'open', then any item which can be shown to be the unique member of its class is fully and unambiguously identified in the grammar. (1963a, 8)

53 . . . a given class breaks down by simple subdivision into a system of more delicate classes, but the same original class will also subdivide in a number of different ways, so that many dimensions of classification intersect with one another. Any given item, to be fully identified, may require to be simultaneously classified on all such dimensions. In this way it can be assigned to a 'microclass', this representing its value in respect of all the properties which have been found relevant to the way it patterns in the language. (1963a, 11)

54 A 'class' is any set of items having the same possibilities of operation in structure; . . . this always means, except in cases of rankshift, 'in the structure of the unit next above'. (1964b, 29)

55 . . . 'class' . . . provides the bridge between grammar and lexis, in the sense that many grammatical classes are . . . made up of items which cannot be fully described in the grammar and must therefore be handled as lexical items. (1964b, 35)

56 No grammar has, it is believed, achieved the degree of delicacy required for the reduction of all /formal/ items to one-member classes, although provided the model can effectively handle cross-classification it is by no means absurd to set this as the eventual aim: that is, a unique description for each item by its assignment to a 'microclass', which represents its value as the product of the intersection of a large number of classificatory dimensions. (1966c, 149)

57 A class is a statement of 'choices now open' . . . (1969/76a, 5)

1.5 Concord

58 Concord is the multiple exponence of grammatical categories . . . (1966d, 180)

1.6 Consists of

59 'Consists of', like 'unit' and 'rank', also belongs to the theory: the realization in form varies between and within language, and is stated of course in description. The possibilities are sequence, inclusion and conflation. Thus, if in a given instance a unit of one rank consists of the unit of rank next below, these may appear in form as one following, interrupting, or overlaying the other. (1961, 251)

1.7 Constituent

60 A constituent is a particular word or phrase in a particular place; but functionally the choice of an item may have one meaning, its repetition another and its location in structure yet another—or many others . . . (1971d, 109)

1.8 Dimension

61 It is useful to stress the multi-dimensional nature of the systematization: a form may be ordered in the language by its being placed in a number of dimensions—that is, by its being assigned as a term to a number of different systems. The choice of assignment, and the hierarchical ordering of the systems to which

9

it is assigned, will depend upon the purpose of the linguist . . . (1956a, 179)

62 . . . the question whether, for example, s(be) is 'one word' or half a dozen 'different words' in Chinese does not arise if one says of a linguistic form that it operates at certain places in certain structures. Such a treatment is possible with a multi-dimensional description according to which a form may be systematized (that is identified as a term in a grammatical system) along a number of different dimensions, sometimes for different purposes. (1956a, 192)

63 Two dimensions of classes are implicit in the taxonomic hierarchy of the unit system: as characteristic of each unit except the lowest there appears the dimension compound/simple, while for each unit except the highest there may be set up the complementary system of free/bound; the free member is exponentially identified with the simple member of the unit next above. (1957, 59)

1.9 Element

---

64 Elements and classes are categories set up to describe units. The elements are structural and will be stated as symbols . . . (1956a, 181)

65 The elements set up to describe the structure of the sentence represent the upper limit of systematization; these in turn determine the limits of the classes, since the class of forms operating at each place in the structure of the sentence is a class of the clause. (1956a, 182)

66 Each element represents the potentiality of operation of a member of one *grouping* of members of the unit next below, considered as one item-grouping. (1961, 256)

67 . . . the element of structure is . . . a complex of structural roles. (1967c, 215)

10

68 Each element of . . . structure is a complex of functions, a set of structural 'roles' specified as realizations of the options selected. (1969a, 255)

69 . . . the element of a structure, the constituent, is a complex of structural functions each of which represents some choice that the speaker has made in the planning of that sentence. (1969/76a, 5)

1.10 Labelling

70 There are two ways of labelling: according to structural function, and according to class. (1969/76a, 5)

71 The two types of labelling . . . as it were face different ways in relation to the concept of choice. (1969/76a, 5)

72 Since structure is fully predictable, being derived from the systemic representation, the primary labels used here are functional ones. (1969/76a, 5)

73 . . . the structural labelling is functional and componential, the element of structure being a complex of functions realizing different options. (1969/76a, 6)

1.11 Morpheme

74 The morpheme is no more and no less 'fundamental', being no more and no less an abstraction, than the sentence. (1961, 286)

75 'Morpheme' is the term used to name the smallest unit in the grammar of any language. (1964b, 25)

1.12 Place

76 Places are distinguished by order alone: . . . (1961, 255)

77 Each place is the place of operation of one member of the unit next below, considered as one occurrence. (1961, 256)

1.13 Sentence

---

78 . . . here 'sentence' is the name given to the largest /unit/ about which grammatical statements are to be made. (1956a, 182)

79 This does not exclude the possibility, and even necessity, of making contextual statements about some larger unit /than the sentence/. Such statements would give meaning at another level to features accounted for in the grammatical statement, and may be required to complete an otherwise partial systematization of the material. One could set up a unit of contextual statement, features of which would determine grammatical features. (1956a, 182)

80 It would seem desirable that ultimately the attempt should be made to set up a unit of description larger than the sentence. Such a unit might show a distribution of sentence classes, in which case it would be discussed in the grammar; alternatively a contextual unit might be shown to display a structure such that some sentences could be said to be contextually bound. (1956a, 184)

81 One may begin /grammatical analysis/ by establishing, and delimiting the exponents of, that unit (which we may call the 'sentence') which, while within the scope of grammatical statement—not so extensive as to be incapable of systemic analysis—is yet enabled to operate as the linguistic action of participants in a situation: which is, in fact, 'living language' and constitutes the unit of analysis at the contextual level. (1957, 58)

82 There will always be one unit which, more than other, offers itself as an item for contextual statement because it does the language work in situations: so it might as well always have the same name: 'sentence'. (1961, 252)

83 The sentence is not the largest pattern-carrying unit in English: some patterns clearly extend above it. . . . At the moment only a very partial account can be given of grammar above the sentence, whereas from the sentence downwards the patterns can be filled in in considerable detail. It may turn out that only a part of the relations above the sentence can be brought within the framework of any grammatical theory. (1964b, 26)

84 . . . the sentence is still significantly the lowest 'non-disorderable' unit; it is the unit with which, as it were, language operates in situations. (1964b, 27)

85 . . . it is doubtful whether it is possible to demonstrate generalized structural relationships into which sentences enter as the realization of function in some higher unit, as can be done for all units below the sentence. (1976b, 10)

1.14 Structure

86 The structure is a syntagmatic framework of interrelated elements, which are paradigmatically established in the systems of classes and stated as values in the structure. (1957, 59)

87 In grammar the category set up to account for likeness between events in successivity is the 'structure'. (1961, 254)

88 If the relation between events in successivity is 'syntagmatic', the structure is the highest abstraction of patterns of syntagmatic relations. (1961, 254)

89 A structure is always a structure *of a given unit*. (1961, 255)

90 A structure is . . . an arrangement of elements ordered in 'places'. (1961, 255)

91 The structure is set up to account for likeness between events of the same rank, and it does so by referring them to the rank next below. (1961, 259)

92 The relation between structure and class is a two-way relation,

13

and there is no question of 'discovering' one 'before' the other . . . all structures presuppose classes and all classes presuppose structure. (1961, 260–61)

93 A structure is an ordered arrangement of elements in chain relation . . . (1963a, 7)

94 By a place-ordered structure I mean one composed of a limited number of *different* elements occuring nonrecursively. Such a structure may be fully class-defining, in the sense that to each element corresponds a distinct class of lower rank . . . (1963a, 11)

95 Language also exhibits a different kind of structure /from the place-ordered/, the 'recursive' or 'depth-ordered' structure. Here, as the name implies, an element of structure, or a combination of elements, is repeated 'in depth', a series of such elements (or combinations) thus forming a progression. It is doubtful whether one should set a theoretical limit to the degree of depth in recursion; rather there appears to be some logarithmic scale of diminishing frequency, so that the number of observations one would expect to have to make before recording a depth of, say, ten would be extremely high. Spoken English seems to tolerate greater depth in recursion, or at least to tolerate it more readily, than written English; and this may be true of language generally. (1963a, 11–12)

96 The category of 'structure' . . . is the category that accounts for the various ways in which an occurrence of one unit may be made up out of occurrence of the unit next below it (including, sometimes, rankshifted occurrences of a unit higher than the one next below it). (1964b, 28)

97 The category of 'structure' applies to all units in the grammar of a language except the smallest, which by definition has no structure since it is not made up of anything smaller that can be identified *at the level of grammar*. (1964b, 28)

98 It is the structure that determines the value that a particular clause has in a sentence, a particular group in a clause, and so on. The different values are accounted for by ELEMENTS of structure . . . (1964b, 28)

99 A structure is a highly generalized statement of the meaningful relations between elements; it is the basic pattern of relationships between the parts of a clause, or a sentence or of any other unit, and thereby determines their value. (1964b, 42)

100 Structure is here regarded as a configuration of syntagmatic functions such that a set of items assuming the functions embodied in a given structure can be said to cohere to form a single item of higher rank; thus, in English, clauses cohere by virtue of their function in sentence structure, likewise groups in clause structure. All structure is in this sense cohesive. (1964/67, 219)

101 By 'structure' we may understand the representation of an item in terms of its constituents, with the linearity that such a representation implies . . . (1969/76a, 4)

102 . . . since the structure is regarded as the realization of systemic choices, the grammar has to indicate how the particular choices made by the speaker are realized in structural terms. (1969/76a, 5)

103 . . . the structural representation of a sentence is derived by realization from the systemic one, so that the latter is the more absract (deeper). (1969/76a, 6)

104 A complete structure is thus a sequence of elements, composed of functions any of which may extend across more than one element . . . (1969/76a, 6)

105 . . . the structural representation is minimally bracketed. (1969/76a, 6)

106 The output of any path through the network of systems is a structure. In other words, the structure is the expression of a set of choices made in the system network. (1974b, 88)

107 Structure refers to the combination of elements one with another:

both this *and* that; whereas the underlying concept of system is one of choice: *either* this *or* that. (1975c, 26)

108 Structure is, of course, a unifying relation. The parts of a sentence or a clause obviously 'cohere' with each other, by virtue of the structure. Hence, they also display texture; the elements of any structure have, by definition, an internal unity which ensures that they all express part of a text. (1976b, 6)

109 Discourse structure is, as the name implies, a type of structure; the term is used to refer to the structure of some postulated unit higher than the sentence, for example the paragraph, or some larger entity such as episode or topic unit. (1976b, 10)

110 . . . the structure of discourse. By this we mean the larger structure that is a property of the forms of discourse themselves . . . (1976b, 326–7)

111 Much of discourse structure involves patterns of reference, ellipsis and the like which lie outside the more restricted conception of linguistic structure and whose range extends across the boundaries of recognized structural units . . . (1967c, 243)

1.15 Unit

---

112 The unit is that category to which corresponds a segment of the linguistic material about which statements are to be made . . . The interrelation among the units is such that each, except the /smallest/ admits a distinction into simple and compound, the simple being that whose structure is stated as a single element while the compound is that of which the structure consists of two or more elements. Since the system of terms operating at a particular place in the structure of a given unit is a system of classes of the unit next below the units form a hierarchy in which each may have as its structural components (that is, as forms operating at places in its structure) either one or more than one form being a term in the class system of the next. (1956a, 180–81)

113 Implicit in the interrelation of elements and classes is the fact that, once the largest unit is defined and structures set up for it, the remaining units are self-defining. (1956a, 181–2)

114 The units are defined by interrelation in terms of extent: unlike a system of classes, whose terms are both collectively exhaustive and mutually exclusive, the single system of units forms a hierarchy in descending progression, such that each term is defined as *n* times the succeeding term, that is, as consisting of one or more members of the succeeding term (exponentially, every exponent of a given unit is statable *either* as (coextensively) a single exponent *or* as a sequence of exponents of the unit next in succession). (1957, 58)

115 A descending order of procedure seems preferable not only for the presentation . . . but also for the analysis of the grammar, where in such a hierarchic progression the classification made at the level of each unit will itself determine the classes that are to be set up for the lower units. (1957, 58)

116 It is probable that in the description of any language at least two units will be required: these would be such as could be named the 'sentence' and the 'word'. (1957, 58)

117 The units are established in the grammar, by formal grammatical criteria, though in the delimitation of exponents of each unit within the text other criteria, phonetic or graphic, may contribute and may be taken, where to do so is compatible with the general aims of simplicity and comprehensiveness, as the primary or even sole criteria . . . (1957, 58)

118 In the subsequent establishment and classification of the lower units /than 'sentence'/, the statements made about each unit will be related to values set up in the structure of the higher unit. (1957, 58)

119 For each unit there will then be set up systems of classes, formally established in the grammar and exhaustive, such that statements may be made which are valid for all exponents of a given unit. (1957, 59)

17

120 Each unit is characterized by certain structures. (1957, 59)

121 The units of the grammar form a hierarchy that is a taxonomy. (1961, 251)

122 . . . each /unit/ 'consists of' one, or more than one of the unit next below . . . (1961, 251)

123 No special status, other than that presupposed by rank, is assigned by grammatical theory to any one unit. (1961, 252)

124 . . . in grammatical theory, all languages have at least two units; in description, all languages have sentences and all languages have words—but the 'sentenceness' of sentences and 'wordness' of the word do not derive from the theory of grammar. (1961, 252)

125 . . . there can be no question of independent identification of the exponents of the different units, since criteria of any given unit always involve reference to others, and therefore indirectly to all the others. (1961, 254)

126 Each unit may display a range of possible structures, and the only theoretical restriction is that each unit must carry at least one structure that consists of more than one place. (1961, 256)

127 . . . even though we may use the categories of 'unit' and 'structure' both in grammar and in phonology, these are not shown to be comparable unless the two theories have the same system of primitive terms with the same inter-relations. (1961, 256n)

128 . . . one must be free to recognize grammatical units whose exponents in substance both overlap with and completely fail to coincide with the units carrying phonological contrasts. (1961, 281)

129 In discussing a grammatical item or category one may thus ask at what *unit* it is operating: where in the language is this particular choice made? The stretches that carry the grammatical patterns are what I am calling 'units'. (1961/66, 7)

130 . . . every language will have at least two grammatical units: indeed this is perhaps one universal feature of languages. We might go so far as to say this: 'All languages have at least two grammatical units: a larger one which is the unit of contextual meaning, the one with which the language operates in situations, and this we call the *sentence*; and a smaller one which is the unit that also mainly enters into lexical relations, and this we call the *word*.' (1961/66, 7)

131 In general the units of a language are related to each other in a hierarchy based on the notion of constituency; each is composed of one or of several members of the unit next below. The term rank is used for the position of the unit in the hierarchy. (1961/66, 7)

132 However many units we recognize in the grammar of any given language there is always a fixed relation among them: an occurrence of any unit is said to consist of one, or more than one, complete occurrence of the unit *next below it*. (1964b, 25)

133 Wherever a grammatical choice is made, there is a unit that carries that choice. (1964b, 25)

134 The unit is the stretch of language that carries grammatical patterns. (1964b, 25)

135 It is a property of all languages that one can recognize units in their grammar, and that these units are built up one inside the other. (1964b, 25)

2
Form

136 The form is the organization of the substance into meaningful events . . . (1961, 243)

137 Formal meaning is the 'information' of information theory, though (i) it can be stated without being quantified and was in fact formulated in linguistics independently of the development of information theory as a means of quantifying it, and (ii) formal meaning in lexis cannot be quantified until a method is found for measuring the information of non-finite ('open') sets. The formal meaning of an item is its operation in the network of formal relations. (1961, 244–5)

138 . . . 'formal item', is a technical term for the endpoint of the exponence relation ('most exponential' point) *in form* . . . (1961, 250n)

139 The grammarian's dream is (and must be, such is the nature of grammar) of constant territorial expansion. He would like to turn the whole of linguistic form into grammar, hoping to show that lexis can be defined as 'most delicate grammar'. The exit to lexis would then be closed, and all exponents ranged in systems. (1961, 267)

140 The ultimate exponent in form is the formal item. (1961, 271)

141 When grammar reaches the formal item, either it has said all there is formally to be said about it or it hands over to lexis. (1961, 271)

142 The formal item is the boundary of grammar on the exponence scale. It is not of course the boundary on the rank scale: whenever the formal item is anything other than a single morpheme . . . the grammar *can* be taken further down in *rank* . . . (1961, 271)

143 It is . . . too often assumed that what cannot be stated *grammatically* cannot be stated *formally*: that what is not grammar is semantics, and here, some would add, linguistics gives up. But the view that the only formal linguistics is grammar might be described as a colourless green idea that sleeps furiously between the sheets of linguistic theory, preventing the bed from being made. What are needed are theoretical categories for the formal description of lexis. (1961, 275)

144 Under 'form', however, we must make a further distinction between *grammar* and *lexis* (vocabulary), a distinction likewise made necessary by the nature of language. In every language the formal patterns are of two kinds, merging into one another in the middle but distinct enough at the extremes: those of grammar and those of vocabulary (or, to use a technical term, of lexis). (1961/66, 4)

145 . . . the formal analysis of language is itself a study of meaning. It is impossible to describe language without taking into account the meaning. We entirely agree with those linguists in demanding formal—that is, linguistic—criteria for linguistic categories: but what we cannot accept is this dichotomy between form and meaning, for it is a false opposition. (1961/66, 40)

146 In grammar and lexis we are accounting for the FORMAL ITEMS of a language. A 'formal item' is any meaningful stretch of language, of any extent. The reason for calling this a 'formal item' instead of simply 'item' is that it is defined within linguistic form and is thus itself the product of a process of abstraction . . . (1964b, 23–4)

147 When we describe the formal features of a language, its grammar and lexis, we are trying to account for all the possible meaningful contrasts that the language makes. (1964b, 42)

148 . . . formal items . . . vary in respect of which of the two kinds of pattern, the grammatical or the lexical, is more significant for the explanation of restrictions on their occurrence qua items. (1966c, 155)

2.2 Form/Function

149 The 'formal/functional' dichotomy is one which linguistics is better rid of; it is misleading to say even that classes are functionally determined, since they are set up with reference to the *form* of the unit next above—the whole description is both formal and functional at the same time, and 'function' is merely an aspect of form. (1961, 261)

150 Syntactic classification (sometimes referred to as 'functional classification', in what is perhaps a rather misleading opposition of 'form' and 'function') . . . (1963a, 5)

151 Form and function are no more opposed to one another than are form and meaning. If we take these terms in the sense in which they are usually used, a linguistic description is both formal and functional. (1964b, 40)

152 There is not a choice between two ways of describing grammar, a formal way and a functional way; the whole framework of unit, structure, system and class is both 'formal' and 'functional' at once. (1964b, 41)

2.3 Initial Position

153 The sequence of elements in the clause tends to represent thematic ordering rather than ordering in transitivity . . . and this is particularly true of the function of clause-initial position which reflects a division of the clause into 'theme' and 'rheme' . . . (1967c, 205)

154 In English there is a definite awareness of the meaning expressed by putting something in first position in the clause. (1970b, 162)

155 . . . there is only one semantically significant place in sequence in the English clause, namely first place. (1970c, 352)

156 Nearly all variation in sequence in the clause is statable in terms of first position. (1970c, 352)

157 First position in the clause . . . is structurally significant: it is the realization of the category of 'theme', which is an element deriving from the textual function of language. (1970c, 357–8)

2.4 Linearity

158 It is obvious that *absolute* measurements of linear progression belong to language *substance* . . . What is less obvious is that the whole dimension of progression in fact belongs to substance, and that the stretches which carry grammatical patterns—or rather the members of that abstract category that we set up to account for these stretches—have to be ranged on a dimension of which linear progression is only a manifestation in substance: a dimension we may call 'order'. (1961, 250)

159 A structure is made up of 'elements' which are graphically represented as being in linear progression; but the theoretical relation among them is one of 'order'. (1961, 254)

160 . . . it must be stressed that linear progression itself is a feature of substance. (1961, 254)

161 . . . the linear succession of the items does not act as a constant in showing the depth relation . . . (1963a, 14)

162 The systemic representation is then realized as structure, with linear ordering . . . (1969a, 255)

163 The linear arrangement of the parts of a sentence does not figure, here, in the most abstract representation of that sentence; structure is treated as a mechanism whereby the speaker realizes or makes manifest the choices he has made. (1969/76a, 4)

164 . . . the description of a language must at some stage take cognizance of succession in real time; the problem is at what point to introduce linearity into the description. (1969/76a, 4)

2.5 Order

165 Order may, but does not necessarily, have as its realization 'sequence' the formal relation carried by linear progression; sequence is at a lower degree of abstraction than order and is one possible formal exponent of it. (1961, 254–5)

166 . . . there is *order* among the levels, determined by their inter-relations, but (a) no hierarchy, in the *defined* sense of the word, and (b) no procedural direction. (1961, 248n)

167 There is a great overall variation in the permitted ordering of elements; but it seems to follow simply from one general prin-ciple, which is that it must be possible for all elements, and all combinations of elements, to come in first position. (1970c, 352)

168 The ordering of elements in the structure of the English clause is the product of the interaction between these two functions of language /interpersonal and functional/. (1970c, 360)

2.6 Sequence

169 . . . in any given instance sequence may *not* manifest order, or . . . order may have other manifestations . . . (1961, 250–51)

170 . . . sequence is a variable, and must be replaced in the theory by the more abstract dimension of order. (1961, 251)

171 Sequence is presumably always manifested in phonic substance as linear progression; the distinction is then one of exponence, 'sequence' being the name for that formal relation between formal items of which linear progression is the manifestation in phonic substance. (1961, 255n)

172 Sequence is sometimes a structural feature, sometimes not. Or, to put it in other terms, it sometimes happens in a language that to change the sequence of the constituents destroys (or changes) the structure; in other cases a change of sequence has no effect on the primary structure. (1961/66, 11)

173 It is a commonplace of linguistics that on the chain axis, that involving relations of structure, the value of sequence is variable. That is to say, the sequence in which items occur may or may not be a crucial property of the structure in question. (1963a, 8)

174 . . . when we say that sequence 'may or may not be' significant for structure, what we mean is that it may be significant at varying degrees of delicacy, down to a point where a distinction becomes so delicate that we do not know what to say about it; in such cases we may have to be prepared to *treat* the particular feature of sequence as nonsignificant. (1963a, 9)

175 The relation among elements of structure is not the same thing as their arrangement in sequence. (1964b, 28)

2.7 Substance

---

176 Language, whether spoken or written, has a substance: this is the material aspect of language. The substance may be phonic or graphic . . . The noise, then, is the substance. Language also has a form: this is the organization. In language, therefore, we can recognize a level of *substance* and a level of *form*. Now the organization of language, its form, is meaningful: that is, linguistic activity participates in situations alongside man's other creative activities. Thus for a complete description of language one has to account for the form, the substance and the relationship between the form and the situation. The study of this relationship could be called the *semantic* level, but since it involves an approach to meaning rather different from that normally implied by 'semantics' we may refer to this as the 'contextual' level, the 'context' here being the non-linguistic environment. (1961/66, 3–4)

177 The substance is the material of language: 'phonic' (audible noise) or 'graphic' (visible marks). (1961, 243)

178 A grammatical category is *not* required to be identifiable by reference to a particular feature of substance stated phonologically: it merely carries the potentiality of being stated in phonological terms. (1961, 284)

3
Function

3.1 Developmental Functions

179 . . . these functions, namely the instrumental, the regulatory, the interactional, the personal, the heuristic, and the imaginative, represented the developmental functions of language. (1975c, 33)

180 It is presumed that these /developmental functions/ are universals of human culture, and it is not unreasonable to think of them as the starting point not only for linguistic ontogeny but also for the evolution of the linguistic system. (1975c, 33)

3.2 Discoursal Function

181 The /discoursal function/ meets the basic requirement of every language that it should be able to create texts. The speaker of a language can recognize a text; his ability to discriminate between a random string of sentences and one forming a discourse is due to the inherent texture in the language and to his awareness of it. One aspect of the discourse function is thus 'grammar above the sentence', the area often known as 'discourse structure' and concerned with the options that are available to the speaker for relating one sentence to another. But the discoursal function of language embodies also the means whereby what is said may be structured as a piece of communication, and this involves grammar below the sentence. The construction of discourse demands resources not only for attaching a sentence to what has

27

preceded it but also for organizing the sentence in such a way that it is appropriate as information in the context. (1968a, 210)

182 The discoursal component provides, through the encoding equative structure, the means for distributing the experiential functions in every possible way over the functions theme–rheme and given–new . . . (1968a, 215)

3.3 Experiential Function

183 The term 'experiential' makes it clear that the underlying function is seen not as the expression of 'reality' or 'the outer world' but as the expression of patterns of experience; the content given to an utterance by this portion of the language system derives from the shared experience of those participating in the speech situation. (1968a, 209)

184 The experiential component could be referred to as a 'content' component, were it not that this calls to mind the form/content opposition, which is irrelevant in the present context. (1968a, 209)

185 The *experiential* function, as the name implies, is the 'content' function of language: it is language as the expression of the processes and other phenomena of the external world, including the world óf the speaker's own consciousness, the world of thoughts, feelings, and so on. (1974b, 95)

186 . . . experiential, /function/ representing the linguistic interpretation of experience . . . (1976b, 238)

3.4 Functional Approach

187 We are concerned . . . with a functional theory that is both general and linguistic. (1970c, 324)

188 The essential feature of a functional theory is not that it enables us to enumerate and classify the functions of speech acts, but that it provides a basis for explaining the nature of the language system, since the system itself reflects the functions that it has evolved to serve. (1971a, 65–6)

189 By a functional theory of language I mean one which attempts to explain linguistic structure, and linguistic phenomena, by reference to the notion that language plays a certain part in our lives; that it is required to serve certain universal types of demand. (1971d, 104)

190 A functional theory of language is a theory about meanings, not about words or constructions . . . (1971d, 110)

191 What do we understand by a 'functional approach' to the study of language? . . . Among other things, it would be helpful to be able to establish some general principles relating to the use of language; and this is perhaps the most usual interpretation of the concept of a functional approach. (1973a, 22)

192 The ability to speak and understand, and the development of this ability in the child, are essential ingredients in the life of social man. To approach these from the outside, as interorganism phenomena, is to take a functional view of language. The social aspect of language becomes the reference point for the biological aspect, rather than the other way round. (1974a, 12)

193 . . . we are taking a functional view of language, in the sense that we are interested in what language can do, or rather in what the speaker, child or adult, can do with it; and that we try to explain the nature of language, its internal organization and patterning, in terms of the functions that it has evolved to serve. (1974a, 13)

194 A functional theory is not a theory about the mental processes involved in the learning of the mother tongue; it is a theory about the social processes involved. (1974a, 15)

195 From the functional point of view, as soon as there are meaningful expressions there is language . . . (1975c, 6)

196 This is part of the significance of the functional approach: it provides a criterion for identifying what is language and what is not. (1975c, 22)

3.5 Function/Use

---

197 We . . . need to make a distinction, in the adult language system, between 'function' and 'use', a distinction which was unnecessary in the case of the child's proto-language. With the child, each use of language has its own grammar from which we can (in the idealized original state of the system) fully derive the structures and items employed in that use.

With the adult this is not so. He may use language in a vast number of different ways, in different types of situation and for different purposes; but we cannot identify a finite set of uses and write a grammar for each of them. What we can identify, however, is a finite set of functions—let us call them 'macro-functions' to make the distinction clearer—which are general to all these uses and through which the meaning potential associated with them is encoded into grammatical structures. (1972a, 98–9)

198 With the very young child, 'function' equals 'use'; and there is no grammar, no intermediate level of internal organization in language, only a content and expression. With the adult, there are indefinitely many uses but only three or four functions, or 'macro-functions' as we are calling them; and these macro-functions appear at a new level in the linguistic system—they take the form of 'grammar'. (1974a, 36)

199 . . . I would like to make a distinction between *function* and *use* . . . As far as the adult language is concerned, it is possible to talk about the 'uses' of language, by which I would understand simply the selection of options within the linguistic system in the context of actual situation types: 'uses' in its informal everyday sense. In that sense, use is a valuable concept; but we can't really enumerate the uses of language in a very systematic way—the nearest we can come to that is some concept of situation types, of which Bernstein's critical socializing contexts would be an example. Now I would distinguish that from function, because the whole of the adult language is organized around a small number of functional components . . . Now what are these components? Fundamentally, they are the components of the language system which correspond to the abstract functions of language—to what I have called 'meta-functions', areas of meaning potential which are inherently involved in all uses of language. These are what I am referring to as ideational, inter-personal, and textual; generalized functions which have as it were become built into language, so that they form the basis of the organization of the entire linguistic system. (1974b, 93–4)

3.6 Given/New

200 . . . the elements of the clause structure are contextually distributed in a system of 'given/new' . . . (1956a, 188)

201 The 'given' is defined as a term already present in the context of situation . . . (1956a, 188)

202 . . . the contextual categories of given and new may aid in the identification of grammatical categories: a certain category might be identified as the form taken by the given or that taken by the new. (1957, 62)

203 The functions 'given' and 'new' are . . . not the same as those of 'theme' and 'rheme'. The two are independently variable . . . (1967c, 205)

204 . . . the given–new structure is not itself realized by the sequence of elements . . . (1967c, 205)

205 . . . the partial congruence between /given–new/ and . . . theme–rheme together with the partial congruence between clause and information unit, results in a tendency towards a left to right form of organization in the information unit with given, if present, preceding new. (1967c, 205)

206 /Given and new/ are options on the part of the speaker, not determined by the textual or situational environment; what is new is in the last resort what the speaker chooses to present as new, and predictions from the discourse have only a high probability of being fulfilled. (1967c, 211)

207 The constituent specified as new is that which the speaker marks out for interpretation as non-derivable information, either cumulative to or contrastive with what has preceded; the given is offered as recoverable anaphorically or situationally. (1967c, 211)

208 The function 'given' means 'treated by the speaker as non-recoverable information': information that the listener is not being expected to derive for himself from the text or the situation. (1970b, 163)

209 Given and new thus differ from theme and rheme, though both are textual functions, in that 'given' means 'here is a point of contact with what you know' (and thus is not tied to elements in clause structure), whereas 'theme' means 'here is the heading to what I am saying'. (1970b, 163)

210 This part of the message, which we shall call the 'given', has a specific function in the textual organization: it links the information unit to the rest of the discourse. (1970c, 354)

211 By the 'given' we understand that part of the message which is shown, in English by intonation, to constitute a link in the chain of discourse. (1970c, 354)

212 For every unit of the message . . . there is one part, not necessarily corresponding to a constituent of any other kind, that the speaker signals as being 'new': that is, that he explicitly offers as non-recoverable information. (1970c, 354)

213 While given–new is a structure not of the clause but of the information unit, and is realized not by sequence but by intonation, theme–rheme on the other hand is a structure of the clause, and is realized by the sequence of elements: the theme comes first. (1970c, 356)

214 . . . the given is hearer-oriented and context-bound, whereas the theme is speaker-oriented and context-free. (1970c, 357)

215 The Given element is optional; the New is present in every information unit, since without it there would not be a separate information unit. (1976b, 326)

3.7 Heuristic Function

---

216 . . . the child has a HEURISTIC model of language, derived from his knowledge of how language has enabled him to explore his environment . . . The heuristic model refers to language as a means of investigating reality, a way of learning about things. (1969b, 14)

217 The heuristic is the use of language to learn, to explore reality: the function of 'tell me why'. (1969b, 17)

218 . . . the *heuristic* function . . . is language as means of exploring the environment, the 'tell me why' function of language . . . (1974b, 110–11)

3.8 Ideational Function

---

219 Language serves for the expression of 'content': that is, of the speaker's experience of the real world, including the inner world of his own consciousness. We may call this the *ideational* function, though it may be understood as easily in behavioural as in conceptual terms. In serving this function, language also gives structure to experience, and helps to determine our way of looking at things, so that it requires some intellectual effort to see them in any other way than that which our language suggests to us. (1970b, 143)

220 To the adult—though not, be it noted, to the child—the predominant demand that we make on our language (predominant, at least, in our thinking about language; perhaps that is all) is that it allows us to communicate about something. We use language to represent our experience of the processes, persons, objects, abstractions, qualities, states and relations of the world around us and inside us. Since this is not the only demand we make on language it is useful to refer to it specifically; hence 'ideational function', 'ideational meaning' etc. (other terms that have been used in a similar sense are 'representational', 'cognitive', 'semantic', 'factual-notional' and 'experiential'). (1970b, 145–6)

221 In the first place language serves for the expression of content: it has a representational, or, as I would prefer to call it, an *ideational* function . . . Two points need to be emphasized concerning this ideational function of language. The first is that it is through this function that the speaker or writer embodies in language his experience of the phenomena of the real world; and this includes his experience of the internal world of his own consciousness: his reactions, cognitions and perceptions, and also his linguistic acts of speaking and understanding . . . There is, however, and this is the second point, one component of ideational meaning which, while not unrelatable to experience, is nevertheless organized in language in a way that marks it off as distinct: this is the expression of certain fundamental logical relations such as are encoded in language in the form of co-ordination, apposition, modification and the like . . . Within the ideational function of language, therefore, we can recognize two sub-functions, the *experiential* and the *logical* . . . (1971d, 106)

222 The ideational component is that part of the grammar concerned with the expression of experience, including both the processes within and beyond the self—the phenomena of the external world and those of consciousness—and the logical relations deducible from them. The ideational component thus has two sub-components, the experiential and the logical. (1972a, 99)

223 For the child, the use of language to inform is just one instance of language use, one function among many. But with the adult, the ideational element in language is present in all its uses; no matter what he is doing with language he will find himself exploiting its ideational resources, its potential for expressing a content in terms of the speaker's experience and that of the speech community. (1973a, 37)

224 . . . there are the *ideational* options, those relating to the content of what is said. With this component, the speaker expresses his experience of the phenomena of the external world, and of the internal world of his own consciousness. This is what we might call the *observer* function of language, language as a means of talking about the real world. It also includes a subcomponent concerned with the expression of logical relations which are first perceived and interpreted by the child as relations between things. (1975c, 17)

3.9 Imaginative Function

---

225 From his ability to create, through language, a world of his own making /the child/ derives the IMAGINATIVE model of language . . . (1969b, 15)

226 The imaginative function is that of 'let's pretend', whereby the reality is created, and what is being explored in the child's own mind, including language itself. (1969b, 17)

227 . . . the *imaginative* function, 'let's pretend', which is really language for the creation of an environment of one's own. (1974b, 111)

228 . . . we have the *imaginative* function, which is the function of language whereby the child creates an environment of his own . . . This we may call the 'let's pretend' function of language. (1975c, 20)

3.10 Information

229 Any text in spoken English is organized into what may be called 'information units'. (1967c, 200)

230 The distribution of information units represents the speaker's blocking out of the message into quanta of information, or message blocks. (1967c, 202)

231 The information unit is what the speaker chooses to encode as a unit of discourse . . . (1967c, 202)

232 The distribution of the discourse into information units . . . represents a distinct dimension of structural organization, one that is not derivable from other syntactic features. (1967c, 203)

233 . . . the system of information focus assigns to the information unit a structure in terms of the two functions 'given' and 'new'. (1967c, 204)

234 Information structure is one aspect of the thematic organization of discourse . . . 1967c, 205)

235 Information is a discourse pattern in the sense that, although the speaker is operating, here as elsewhere in the grammar, with a wide range of options, the factors that he takes into account in exercising these options are those of the textual environment, the preceding discourse; information is thus closely bound up with cohesive patterns such as those of substitution and reference. (1967c, 211)

236 The information systems, in other words, specify a structural unit and structure it in such a way as to relate it to the preceding discourse whereas thematization takes a unit of sentence structure, the clause, and structures it in a way that is independent of what has gone before. (1967c, 212)

237 Within each information unit the speaker selects one, or at most two, points of information focus; phonologically the information unit is realized as a tone group and the information focus as the tonic component. This assigns a structure in terms of an obligatory new element, defined as that which is within the domain of the information focus, optionally accompanied by an element with the function 'given'. (1967c, 243)

238 /Information structure/ refers to the organization of a text in terms of the functions 'given' and 'new'. These are often conflated with theme and rheme under the single heading 'topic and comment'; the latter, however, is (like the traditional notion of 'subject') a complex notion, and the association of theme with given, rheme with new, is subject to the usual 'good reason' principle . . . —there is freedom of choice, but the theme will be associated with the 'given' and the rheme with the 'new' unless there is good reason for choosing some other alignment. (1970b, 162)

239 The information unit consists of an obligatory 'new' element— there must be something new, otherwise there would be no information—and an optional 'given' element . . . (1970b, 163)

240 The mapping of information structure onto clause structure is a distinct relation with its own significance as a semantic variable. (1970c, 356)

241 While the information unit structure, in terms of given and new, gives the message coherence with what has gone before, the organization of the clause into theme and rheme gives it coherence within itself. (1970c, 357)

242 All text in spoken English is organized in information units, and the information unit is structured as a configuration of 'given' and 'new' elements. The realization of this structure involves intonation and rhythm, the upper reaches of the phonological hierarchy . . . (1970c, 354)

243 The information unit is a structural unit, although it cuts across the hierarchy of structural units of constituents in the grammar . . . (1976b, 27)

3.11 Informative Function

244   . . . the *informative* function of language, the 'I've got something to tell you' function. The idea that language can be used as a means of communicating information to someone who does not already possess that information is a very sophisticated one which depends on the internalization of a whole complex set of linguistic concepts that the young child does not possess. It is the only purely intrinsic function of language, the only use of language in a function that is definable solely by reference to language. (1975c, 21)

245   /the informative function/ is an intrinsic function which the child cannot begin to master until he has grasped the principle of dialogue, which means until he has grasped the fundamental nature of the communication process. (1975c, 31)

3.12 Instrumental Function

246   Perhaps the simplest of the child's models of language, and one of the first to be evolved, is what we may call the INSTRUMENTAL model. The child becomes aware that language is used as a means of getting things done . . . Language is brought in to serve the function of 'I want', the satisfaction of material needs. (1969a, 12)

247   In its instrumental function, language is used for the satisfaction of material needs; this is the 'I want' function. (1969b, 17)

248   One of the earliest uses of language that the child explores is an instrumental one: language used for the satisfaction of his material and emotional needs. (1970c, 322)

249   . . . the instrumental function of language. This refers to the use of language for the purpose of satisfying material needs: it is the 'I want' function, including of course 'I don't want'. (1973a, 27)

250   The *instrumental* function is the function that language serves of satisfying the child's material needs, of enabling him to obtain the goods and services that he wants. This is the 'I want' function of language . . . (1975c, 19)

3.13 Interactional Function

251 . . . /one/ of the models that we may postulate as forming part of the child's image of language is the INTERACTIONAL model. This refers to the use of language in the interaction between the self and others. (1969b, 13)

252 The interactional function is that of getting along with others, the 'me and you' function (including 'me and my mummy'). (1969b, 17)

253 The *interactional* function is what we might gloss as the 'me and you' function of language. This is the language used by the child to interact with those around him . . . (1975c, 19)

254 . . . the 'ritual' model of language. This is the image of language internalized by those for whom language is a means of showing how well one was brought up; it downgrades language to the level of table-manners. The ritual element in the use of language is probably derived from the interactional, since language in its ritual function also serves to define and delimit a social group; but it has none of the positive aspects of linguistic interaction . . . (1969b, 16–17)

3.14 Interpersonal Function

255 In addition to the well-described speech functions, statement, question and answer, command and exclamation, the interpersonal component includes such options as those of 'speaker's comment', on the probabilities, the degree of relevance, etc., of the message, and of speaker's attitude (for example confirmation, reservation, contradiction). These options provide a means for the expression of the linguistic roles that can be occupied by the speaker in a communication situation. (1968a, 210)

256 Language serves to establish and maintain social relations; for the expression of social roles, which include the communication roles created by the language itself—for example the roles of questioner or respondent, which we take on by asking or answering a question; and also for getting things done, by means of the interaction between one person and another. Through this function, which we refer to as *interpersonal*, social groups are delimited, and the individual is identified and reinforced, since by enabling him to interact with others language also serves in the expression and development of his own personality. (1970b, 143)

257 Speaker's comment is . . . one among the syntactic complexes which together make up the interpersonal or 'social role' component in language. (1970c, 355)

258 The interpersonal function includes all kinds of commentary by the speaker . . . (1970c, 350)

259 . . . the interpersonal /function/ . . ., language as the mediator of role, including all that may be understood by the expression of our own personalities and personal feelings on one hand, and forms of interaction and social interplay with other participants in the communication situation on the other hand. (1971a, 66)

260 In the second place, language serves what we may call an *interpersonal* function. This is quite different from the expression of content. Here, the speaker is using language as a means of his own intrusion into the speech event: the expression of his comments, his attitudes and evaluations, and also of the relationship that he sets up between himself and the listener—in particular, the communication role that he adopts, of informing, questioning, greeting, persuading and the like. (1971d, 106)

261 The interpersonal component is the grammar of personal participation; it expresses the speaker's role in the speech situation, his personal commitment and his interaction with others. (1972a, 99)

262 . . . there is the *interpersonal* component of the semantic system, reflecting the function of language as a means whereby the speaker participates in the speech situation. This we may call the *intruder* function of language. (1975c, 17)

263 The interpersonal is the potential of the system for the speaker as an intruder: it is the participatory function of language, language as doing something. (1975c, 126–7)

264 The INTERPERSONAL component is concerned with the social, expressive and conative functions of language, with expressing the speaker's 'angle': his attitudes and judgements, his encoding of the role relationships in the situation, and his motive in saying anything at all. (1976b, 26–7)

3.15 Logical Function

265 The logical component provides for the linguistic expression of such universal relations as those of 'and', 'or', negation and implication; and presumably it also underlies the subject–predicate structure of the clause, although this is derivable from another source. (1968a, 209–10)

266 The *logical* component is distinguished in the linguistic system by the fact that it is expressed through recursive structures whereas all the other functions are expressed through non-recursive structures. (1974b, 95)

3.16 Macro-functions

267 The clause is of interest because it provides, perhaps in all languages, a point of intersection of three sets of options . . . associated with experiential meaning, speech function and discourse organization. These three are interrelated in complex ways, and each of them may be found to shed light on the other two. (1967c, 243)

268 . . . /the/ plurality of language function is reflected in the

41

system, and different parts of the system realize different functions; not in the sense that a given sentence has one function and is therefore specified exclusively by one component of the system, but in the sense that, while every sentence expresses a combination of functions and thus all parts of the system have contributed to its specification, it is possible to formulate the contribution made by each part. (1968a, 207)

269 If we represent the set of options available to the speaker in the grammar of the English clause, these options group themselves into a small number of subsets, distinct from one another in that, while within each group of options there is a very high degree of interdependence, between any two groups the amount of interdependence, though by no means negligible, is very much less. This provides a syntactic basis for the concept of language functions, and suggests how the diversity of functions recognizable at the semantic levels may be organized in the course of realization. (1968a, 207)

270 It seems possible to set up four components in the grammar of English representing four functions that the language as a communication system is required to carry out: the experiential, the logical, the discoursal and the speech-functional or interpersonal. In other words the total system of syntactic options appears to fall into four sub-systems which could be labelled in this way. (1968a, 207–9)

271 Perhaps the /component/ that would be thought of as most central is the experiential component: the linguistic expression of the speaker's experience of the external world, including the inner world of his own consciousness—his emotions, perceptions and so on. (1968a, 209)

272 . . . the English clause embodies options of three kinds, experiential, interpersonal and intratextual, specifying relations among (respectively) elements of the speaker's experience, participants defined by roles in the speech situation, and parts of the discourse. Although the clause options do not exhaust the expression of these semantic relations—other syntactic resources

are available, quite apart from the selection of lexical items—the clause provides the domain for many of the principal options associated with these three components. At the same time it is useful to recognize a fourth component, the logical, concerned with the and's and or's and if's of language; this is often subsumed under the first of those above with some general label such as 'cognitive', but it is represented by a specific set of structural resources (hence not figuring among the clause options) and should perhaps rather be considered separately. (1969a, 249)

273 . . . structural function in the clause is fully derivable from systems of options in transitivity, mood and theme. But no one of these sets of options by itself fully specifies the clause structure; each one determines a different set of structural functions. Deriving from options in transitivity are functions such as actor, goal and beneficiary; from modal options, those such as subject, predicator and WH-element; from thematic options, functions such as theme, given and new. (1969a, 249)

274 Let us then suggest four . . . generalized components in the organization of the grammar of a language, and refer to them as components of extralinguistic experience, of speech function, of discourse organization and of logical structure. (1969a, 249)

275 The assignment of clause options to the three components of transitivity, mood and theme reflects their interdependence: there is a relatively high degree of interdependence within each component and a relatively low degree (though not none) between the components. (1969a, 256)

276 A function is a statement of 'choices already made' . . . (1969/76a, 5)

277 Mood, theme and transitivity refer to the organization of the clause in, respectively, its interpersonal, its textual and its experiential function. (1969/76b, 159)

278 The combination of syntactic roles in one element of structure is analogous to the combination of social roles in one individual; it is fundamental to the organization of language, since it is this that enables the various components of language function to combine in the formation of integrated structures. (1969/76b, 160)

279 We cannot say that the structure of the clause is determined by its transitivity pattern, with the other components providing only optional extras. (1969/76b, 169)

280 The speaker does not first decide to express some content and then go on to decide what sort of message to build out of it . . . If he did, the planning of each sentence would be a totally discrete operation and it would be impossible ever to answer a question that had actually been asked. Speech acts involve planning that is continuous and simultaneous in respect of all the functions of language. (1970b, 145)

281 The principle of combining a number of roles in a single complex element of structure is fundamental to the total organization of language, since it is this that makes it possible for the various functions of language to be integrated in one expression. (1970b, 152)

282 The multiple function of language is reflected in linguistic structure; this is the basis for the recognition of the ideational (including logical), interpersonal and textual functions . . . (1970b, 165)

283 The investigation of these functions /ideational, interpersonal, textual/ enables us to relate the internal patterns of language—its underlying options, and their realization in structure—to the demands that are made on language in the actual situations in which it is used. (1970b, 165)

284 It is not necessary to argue that one function is more abstract or 'deeper', than another; all are semantically relevant. (1970b, 165)

285 The functions of language . . . are not different 'levels', in the traditional linguistic sense of the term; nor have they to do with a distinction such as that between a formal system, its interpretation and its use. Rather, the functions are to be understood as generalized uses of language, which, since they seem to determine the nature of the language system, require to be incorporated into our account of that system. (1970c, 325)

286 What needs to be made clear . . . is that it is better claimed that all systematic contrasts in the grammar derive from one or other of these three functions /ideational, interpersonal and textual/. (1970c, 326)

287 Modality and modulation are the same system in different functions . . .; the one is interpersonal, the other ideational. (1970c, 347)

288 . . . there is a semantic region where the two functions, the ideational and the interpersonal, overlap, that of speaker's commentary on comment. (1970c, 349)

289 . . . the two /systems of modality and modulation/ overlap in meaning, and there is the possibility of semantic blends. On the other hand, the two systems are, up to a certain point (in delicacy), formally identical, so that we could in fact set up a single syntactic system . . . which then operates in different functional environments. The system may be entered either from the interpersonal function, in which case it expresses modality, or it may be entered from the ideational function, in which case it expresses modulation. (1970c, 350)

290 . . . /modality and modulation/ are . . . remarkably similar, so that having once taken them apart we have to put them back together again: and this reveals another aspect of the functional diversity, namely that it provides the conditions for bringing together in the grammar what are essentially distinct sets of semantic options. (1970c, 350)

291 The study of language within a social and cultural framework presupposes some account of linguistic functions, and the 'multiple function' view of language has for a long time been familiar in such contexts. (1970c, 360)

292 The macro-functions are the most general categories of meaning potential, common to all uses of language. With only minor exceptions, whatever the speaker is doing with language he will draw on all these components of the grammar. (1972a, 100)

293 . . . functional plurality—that any utterance in the adult language operates on more than one level of meaning at once. This is the crucial difference between the adult language and the child's language. (1974b, 112)

294 . . . the fact that language can serve such a variety of purposes is precisely because the language system is organized into this small set of highly generalized functional components /experiential, interpersonal and textual/. (1974c, 49)

295 Whatever we are using language for, we need to make some reference to the categories of our experience; we need to take on some role of the interpersonal situation; and we need to embody these in the form of text. (1974c, 49–50)

296 What we are calling the functions of language may be regarded as the generalized categories of 'content substance' that the adult use of language requires. (1974c, 51)

297 . . . the functional basis of language is reflected in the nature of constituent structure, which has not merely to serve in the realization of meaning but to accommodate in a single structural realization configurations of elements deriving from different functional points of origin. (1974c, 51)

298 There is an important link between the two senses of 'function', the first as in 'functions in structure' and the second as in 'functions of language': the former, when interpreted semantically, imply the latter. The functional roles that combine to make up a linguistic structure . . . reflect the particular function of language that that structure has evolved to serve . . . (1975c, 5)

299 . . . the semantic system of the adult language is very clearly functional in its composition. It reflects the fact that language has evolved in the service of certain particular human needs. But what is really significant is that this functional principle is carried over and built in to the grammar, so that the internal organization of the grammatical system is also functional in character. (1975c, 16)

300   . . . it appears that each of these different components of meaning /ideational, interpersonal, and textual/ is typically activated by a corresponding component in the semiotic structure of the situation. Thus the *field* is associated with the ideational component, the *tenor* with the *interpersonal* component, and the *mode* with the *textual* component. (1975c, 132)

301   There are three major functional-semantic components, the IDEATIONAL, the INTERPERSONAL and TEXTUAL. (1976b, 26)

3.17 Mood

---

302   Mood represents the organization of participants in speech situations, providing options in the form of speaker roles: the speaker may inform, question or command; he may confirm, request confirmation, contradict or display any one of a wide range of postures defined by the potentialities of linguistic interaction. (1967c, 199)

303   /systems/ of mood express speech function, the relations among the participants in a speech situation and the speech roles assigned by the speaker to himself and his interlocutors . . . (1969a, 248)

304   Mood includes not only the contextual functions of statement, question etc., but also options relating to both the speaker's attitude and comment and to the structure of the predication. (1969a, 256)

305   The term 'mood' refers to a set of related options which give structure to the speech situation and define the relations between speaker and interlocutors in a linguistic interaction. (1969a, 256)

306 . . . every language incorporates options whereby the speaker can vary his own communication role, making assertions, asking questions, giving orders, expressing doubts and so on. The basic 'speech functions' of statement, question, response, command and exclamation fall within this category (though they do not exhaust it), and these are expressed grammatically by the system of *mood*, in which the principal options are declarative, interrogative, (yes/no and WH-types), and imperative etc. (1970b, 159–60)

307 Mood is the grammar of speech functions—the roles adopted (and those imposed on the hearer) by the speaker, and his associated attitudes. This is the interpersonal component . . . (1974c, 50)

308 Perhaps our most purely operational language activity is 'phatic communion', the language of the establishment and maintenance of social relations. (1964b, 91)

3.18 Personal Function

---

309 . . . PERSONAL model. This refers to /the child's/ awareness of language as a form of his own individuality . . . for the child language is very much a part of himself, and the 'personal' model is his intuitive awareness of this, and of the way in which his individuality is identified and realized through language. (1969b, 14)

310 The personal model is related to this: it is the expression of identity, of the self, which develops largely *through* linguistic interaction; the 'here I come' function, perhaps. (1969b, 17)

311 . . . there is the *personal* function. This is the language used to express the child's own uniqueness; to express his awareness of himself, in contradistinction to his environment, and then to mould that self—ultimately, language in the development of personality. . . . We might call this the 'here I come' function of language. (1975c, 20)

3.19 Pragmatic/Mathetic Function

312 Just as we can regard the *pragmatic* use of the new words as arising from the instrumental and regulatory functions, so we can interpret this *mathetic* function as arising primarily from a combination of two others, the personal and the heuristic. (1975c, 28)

313 Essentially, the pragmatic function of the child's transitional phase, Phase II, is that which leads into the interpersonal component of the adult system, while the mathetic leads into the ideational component. (1975c, 29)

3.20 Regulatory Function

314 Closely related to the instrumental model, is the REGULATORY model of language. This refers to the use of language to regulate the behaviour of others. (1969b, 12)

315 The regulatory is the 'do as I tell you' function, language in the control of behaviour. (1969b, 17)

316 . . . the 'regulatory' function of language.
. . . This is the use of language to control the behaviour of others, to manipulate the persons in the environment; the 'do as I tell you' function. (1973a, 31)

317 The *regulatory* function . . . It is the function of language as controlling the behaviour of others, something which the child recognizes very easily because language is used on him in this way . . . The regulatory is the 'do as I tell you' function of language. (1975c, 19)

3.21 Representational Function

318 The representational is the 'I've got something to tell you' function, that of the communication of content. (1969b, 17)

319   . . . the REPRESENTATIONAL model. Language is, in additional to all its other guises, a means of communicating about something, of expressing propositions. The child is aware that he can convey a message in language, a message which has specific reference to the processes, persons, objects, abstractions, qualities, states and relations of the real world around him. (1969b, 16)

320   Among the child's uses of language there appears, after a time, the use of language to convey new information: to communicate a content that is (regarded by the speaker as) unknown to the addressee. I had referred to this in a general way as the 'representational' function; but it would be better, and also more accurate, if one were to use a more specific term, such as 'informative', since this makes it easier to interpret subsequent developments. In the course of maturation this function is increasingly emphasized, until eventually it comes to dominate, if not the adult's use of language, at least his conception of the use of language. (1973a, 35)

3.22 Textual Function

321   . . . language has to provide for making links with itself and with features of the situation in which it is used. We may call this the *textual* function, since this is what enables the speaker or writer to construct 'texts', or connected passages of discourse that is situationally relevant; and enables the listener or reader to distinguish a text from a random set of sentences. (1970b, 143)

322   The textual function is internal to language and is instrumental to the other two /ideational and interpersonal/; it is only because we can select the desired form of the message that we can also use language effectively both to represent an experience and to interact with those around us. (1970c, 326)

323   The textual component is concerned with the creation of text; it expresses the structure of information, and the relation of each part of the discourse to the whole and to the setting. (1972a, 99)

324 Although the textual function differs from the /experiential and the interpersonal/ in that it is intrinsic to language, and thus instrumental and not autonomous, I do not think it should be regarded as restricted to parole, or to the utterance. It is an integral component of the language system, and represents a part of the meaning potential of this system. (1974c, 48)

325 . . . we find a third set of systems . . . concerned with the grammar of messages—the status of the clause and its parts as 'units of communication'. This is the textual component of clause structure . . . (1974c, 50)

326 . . . the textual component is not a 'level' in the usual (stratal) sense of the term; it is a 'vertical' division within the content plane. There is no suggestion of one component being 'deeper' or 'more surface' than another. (1974c, 52)

327 . . . the textual component differs from the others in that, while they are directly relatable to the conditions of language use, the textual component is related only indirectly, through its function of creating text. (1974c, 52)

328 . . . the textual component also incorporates patterns of meaning which are realized outside the hierarchical organization of the system. One of these is INFORMATION structure, which is the ordering of the text, independently of its construction in terms of sentences, clauses and the like, into units of information on the basis of the distinction into GIVEN and NEW . . . (1976b, 27)

329 There is a third component, the TEXTUAL, which is the text-forming component in the linguistic system. This comprises the resources that language has for creating text . . . for being operationally relevant, and cohering within itself and with the context of situation. (1976b, 27)

330 The textual component as a whole is the set of resources in a language whose semantic function is that of expressing relationship to the environment. (1976b, 299)

3.23 Theme

331 . . . /in Theme/ structural function is function in communication, and one of the functions is itself labelled 'theme', so that the term 'theme' is being used both as a general name and as the name for a particular role in the distribution of information in the clause as message . . . (1967c, 200)

332 Theme is concerned with the information structure of the clause; with the status of the elements not as participants in extralinguistic processes but as components of a message; with the relation of what is being said to what has gone before in the discourse, and its internal organization into an act of communication. (1967c, 199)

333 Thematization . . . assigns to the clause a structure in terms of the functions 'theme' and 'rheme'. (1967c, 211–12)

334 . . . the grammar of the English clause includes a set of options whereby the speaker organizes his act of communication as a component of a discourse. It is this set of options that is referred to . . . as 'theme', in the general sense in which it is being contrasted with two other sets of clause options, those of transitivity and mood. (1967c, 241–2)

335 Theme is related to the discoursal, or informational, component; under this heading are brought together the principal options whereby the speaker introduces structure into the discourse and (in the ideal case) ensures 'comprehension'—the recognition of the text as a text, and its interpretation along predicted lines. (1968a, 179)

336 Theme . . . concerns the structuring of the act of communication within the total framework of a discourse, the delimitation of message units and the distribution of information within them. (1969a, 249)

337 Thematic structure is closely linked to another aspect of the textual organization of language, which we may call 'information structure'. (1970b, 162)

338 The thematic function . . . gives the clause its significance as a component of a text. (1970c, 357)

339 The function of theme can be regarded, by a further extension, as the diectic element in the structure of the clause, in that it defines the speaker's angle on the content . . . (1970c, 357)

340 The theme is what turns an ideational structure into a message . . . (1970c, 357)

341 The organization of the clause into a theme and a rheme is a structural feature which, like other structural features, derives from semantic options: it is a configuration of functions expressing·a particular component in the total meaning of the clause, namely the 'textual' component, its meaning as a message. (1970c, 360)

3.24 Theme/Rheme

342 . . . in the clause theme always precedes rheme, the theme–rheme structure being in fact realized by the sequence of elements within the clause . . . (1967c, 205)

343 The theme is what is being talked about, the point of departure for the clause as a message: and the speaker has within certain limits the option of selecting any element in the clause as thematic. (1967c, 212)

344 Basically, the theme is what comes first in the clause; and while this means that . . . there is in the unmarked case (i.e. if the information structure is unmarked) an association of the theme with the given, the two are independent options. The difference can perhaps be best summarized by the observation that, while 'given' means 'what you were talking about' (or 'what I was talking about before'), 'theme' means 'what am I talking about' (or 'what I am talking about now'); and, as any student of rhetoric knows, the two do not necessarily coincide. (1967c, 212)

345 The theme may be an item which is recoverable from the preceding discourse but is not necessarily so; the selection is independent of the context. (1967c, 242)

346 The meaning of theme is not the same as given, although the two functions are often realized by the same elements, or overlapping elements. (1970c, 356)

347 The theme is . . . a function in clause structure, like the subject or the actor. It is in fact what is meant by the psychological subject once the notion of 'given' is abstracted therefrom. (1970c, 356)

348 What the speaker puts first is the theme of the clause, the remainder being 'rheme'. (1970c, 356)

349 In principle, the theme is the point of departure—the takeoff point of the clause; and the significant fact about it is that the speaker is free to select whatever theme he likes. (1970c, 356, 357)

350 The thematic function as such is peculiar to the clause. It may nevertheless be relatable to a more general meaning of first position in English, since in both the verbal group and the nominal group first position realizes a structural function which relates to 'speaker-now' . . . (1970c, 357)

3.25 Transitivity

351 Transitivity is the set of options relating to cognitive content, the linguistic representation of extralinguistic experience, whether of the phenomena of the external world or of feeling, thoughts and perceptions. (1967c, 199)

352 Transitivity is defined as relating to the experiential component of meaning (or 'cognitive', though this term is not really appropriate since all components involve a cognitive stratum) . . . (1968a, 179)

353 . . . transitivity . . . refers to the 'content', or factual-notional structure of the clause in its entirety. (1969/76b, 159)

354 Transitivity is the representation in language of PROCESSES, the PARTICIPANTS therein, and the CIRCUMSTANTIAL features associated with them. 1969/76b, 159)

355 The linguistic expression of processes, and of the participants (and, by extension, the circumstances) associated with them, is known by the general term *transitivity*. (1970b, 148)

356 Transitivity comes under what we have called the 'ideational' function of language. (1970b, 148)

357 Transitivity is the set of options whereby the speaker encodes his experience of the process of the external world, and of the internal world of his own consciousness, together with the participants in these processes and their attendant circumstances . . . (1971d, 134)

358 Transitivity is really the cornerstone of the semantic organization of experience . . . (1971d, 134)

359 Now what does transitivity mean? I understand it to mean the grammar of processes; that is to say, the set of options whereby the speaker expresses the whole range of types of process that are recognized in the semantic system of the language . . . (1974b, 103)

360 Transitivity is the grammar of processes—of actions, mental processes, relations—and the participants in these processes, and the attendant circumstances. This is the experiential component . . . (1974c, 50)

4
Grammar/Lexis

4.1 Grammar

361 The statement is grammatical: that is to say, it is not contextual, lexical or phonological. It both presupposes and contributes to a complete description at all levels, and facts stated at other levels are taken into account. In particular the level of context, which is the level at which extra-linguistic phenomena come into the attention of linguistics, will be referred to in the consideration of the grammatical reflection of contextual categories. (1956a, 179)

362 Some prior phonological analysis is implied in any grammatical description . . . (1956a, 179–80)

363 Possibly, . . . we should not impose a strict demarcation between identification of grammatical terms on grammatical and on non-grammatical (e.g. contextual) criteria. (1957, 64)

364 Grammar is that level of linguistic form at which operate closed systems. (1961, 246)

365 It is not necessary to add a separate criterion of 'simplicity', since this is no use unless defined; and it would then turn out to be a property of a maximally grammatical description, since complication equals a weakening of the power of the theory and hence less grammaticalness. (1961, 246n)

366 . . . the grammar cannot be made to define the units for phonological statements. (1961, 256n)

367 . . . the aim of grammar is to stay in grammar: to account for as much as can possibly be accounted for grammatically, by reference to the categories of grammatical theory. This, since it implies maximum generalization and abstraction, means that one proceeds from category to exponent *by the longest route* that is compatible with never going over the same step twice. (1961, 265)

368 . . . /when/ the description yields a system in which the formal exponents themselves operate as terms . . . we have gone all the way in grammar; the formal items are grammatically contrastive (and do not belong in the dictionary). (1961, 266)

369 The theoretical place of the move from grammar to lexis is . . . not a feature of rank but one of delicacy. It is defined theoretically as the place where increase in delicacy yields no further systems: this means that in description it is constantly shifting as delicacy increases. (1961, 267)

370 So instead of throwing up the grammatical sponge and moving out to lexis while this is still avoidable, the description takes successive steps down the exponence scale, changing rank where necessary, until (at the degree of delicacy chosen) it is brought unavoidably face to face with the formal item. (1961, 271)

371 What do we mean by grammar? The most fruitful criterion seems to be this: when we are dealing with a *closed system* we are concerned with grammar. A *closed system* is a series of terms with the following characteristics:
    1. The list of terms is exhaustive—it contains (say) *a*, *b*, *c* and no more;
    2. each term excludes all the others—if *a*, then not *b* and not *c*;
    3. one cannot create new terms, if *a*, *b*, *c* then one cannot add a *d*.
To be more exact, as one can always imagine the creation of new terms and their integration into a grammatical system the third condition should rather be formulated thus: (3) if a new term is added, at least one of the previous terms undergoes a change of meaning, so that in effect a new system replaces the old. (1961/66, 5–6)

372 Another way of drawing the same distinction between grammar and lexis is to say that grammar is 'deterministic' by contrast with lexis which is 'probabilistic'; in the sense that in grammar one can distinguish what is possible from what is impossible (before assigning probabilities, if one wishes, to what is possible), whereas in lexis one can only distinguish between what is more and what is less probable. (1963a, 8n)

373 . . . items that are fully grammatical (i.e. reducible to one-member classes by successive steps in delicacy . . .) (1963a, 10)

374 Grammar is concerned with choices of the first kind, where there is a small fixed number of possibilities and a clear line between what is possible and what is not. The second kind of choice /'a very large number of possibilities'/ is the domain of lexis. These two types of choice are known respectively as 'closed' and 'open'. (1964b, 22)

375 . . . we cannot account for both patterns of the grammatical type and patterns of the lexical type with the same categories and relations. (1964b, 22)

376 . . . grammar deals with closed system choices, which may be between items ('this/that', 'I/you/he/she/we/they') or between categories (singular/plural, past/present/future); lexis with open set choices which are always between items ('chair/settee/bench/stool' etc.) (1964b, 23)

377 In grammar, we can always fully describe the distinctions between *classes* of items . . . But we cannot always, in grammar, describe fully the distinctions between *items* . . . Here then we leave grammar, and move over to the other formal level, that of lexis. (1964b, 32–3)

378 . . . grammatical regularity in the form of structural parallelism is under certain circumstances cohesive, when it is reinforced by lexical cohesion, or, in verse, by the metric pattern. (1964/67, 220)

379 . . . there is a definable sense in which 'more abstraction' is involved in grammar than is possible in lexis. (1966c, 153)

380 . . . in grammar a 'bridge' category is required between element of structure and term in system on the one hand and formal item on the other; this is the class. In lexis no such intermediate category is required: the item is directly referable to the categories of collocation and set. (1966c, 153)

381 It is not suggested that . . . non-coextensiveness between the items of grammar and those of lexis is the norm, but merely that for certain purposes it is useful to have a descriptive model of language that allows for it. (1966c, 154)

382 The 'most grammatical' item is one which is optimally specifiable grammatically, this can be thought of as 'reducible to a one-member class by the minimum number of steps in delicacy'. Such an item may or may not be 'least lexical' in the sense that there is no collocational environment in which its probability of occurrence deviates significantly from its unconditioned probability. (1966c, 155–6)

383 The system network is the grammar. (1969/76a, 3)

384 The grammar of any language can be represented as a very large network of systems, an arrangement of options in simultaneous and hierarchical relationship. (1969/76a, 3)

385 . . . grammar is the weaving together of strands from the various components of meaning into a single fabric that we call linguistic structure. (1970c, 336)

386 We do not usually find a significant option in behaviour represented straightforwardly in the grammatical system; it is only in odd instances that what the speaker 'can do' is coded immediately as what he 'can say'. There is a level of 'can mean' between the two. (1971a, 57)

387 Grammar is the level at which the various strands of meaning

59

potential are woven into a fabric; or, to express this non-metaphorically, the level at which the different meaning selections are integrated so as to form structures. (1972a, 93)

388 Grammar is the level of formal organization in language; it is a purely internal level of organization, and is in fact the main defining characteristic of language. But it is not arbitrary. Grammar evolved as 'content form': as a representation of the meaning potential through which language serves its various social functions. The grammar itself has a functional basis. (1972a, 98)

389 What we know as 'grammar' is the linguistic device for hooking up together the selections in meaning which are derived from the various functions of language, and realizing them in a unified structural form. (1973a, 42)

390 Grammar means lexicogrammar; that is, it includes vocabulary. (1974b, 86)

391 . . . /grammar/ is the purely internal level of organization, the core of the linguistic system. (1974b, 90)

392 . . . /grammar/ can be defined theoretically, in that the lexicogrammatical system is the level of internal organization of language, the network of relations of linguistic form. (1974b, 90)

393 Grammatical structure may be regarded, in fact, as the means whereby the various components of meaning, deriving from the different functions of language, are integrated together. (1974c, 49)

394 Grammatical structure is a device which enables the speaker to be both observer and intruder at the same time; it is a form of polyphony in which a number of melodies unfold simultaneously, one semantic 'line' from each of the functional components. With a grammar one is free to mean two things at once. (1975c, 30)

395 The distinction between grammatical and lexical is really only one of degree . . . (1976b, 6)

396 . . . a grammatical item (member of a closed system). (1976b, 274)

397 . . . there is no very sharp line between grammar and vocabulary: the vocabulary, or lexis, is simply the open-ended and most 'delicate' aspect of the grammar of a language. (1976b, 281)

4.2 Lexis

398 The words (the units of lexical statement) of the text function in interrelations of collocation and in 'ordered series'; grammatical forms are ranged as terms in paradigmatic systems and operate in syntagmatic relations in the structure. The comprehensive statement of such relations is the statement of the meaning of the text at these levels. (1959, 10)

399 . . . lexical series, defined as groups of words having in common some feature or features of lexical context. (1959, 160)

400 The item for lexical statement is *not* to be identified on the grammatical rank scale; nor is it a 'unit' at all in the sense in which the term is here used in grammar, since this use presupposes a rank scale (as well as the other terms 'structure', 'class', and 'system' in a system of related categories), which is absent from lexis. (1961, 252n)

401 . . . /when/ the description yields a class where no further breakdown by grammatical categories is possible, a class whose exponents make up an open set . . . we must leave grammar; the relations between the exponents must be accounted for as lexical relations. (1961, 266)

402 The exit to lexis tends to be associated predominantly—but probably never uniquely—with one unit, which for this reason is called in description the 'word'. (1961, 266)

403 Once /the word/ has been taken over by lexis, the grammatical categories, and the grammatical exponence scale, no longer impinge on it. (1961, 272)

404 . . . there is no one/one correspondence in exponence between the item which enters into lexical relations and any one of the grammatical units. It is for this reason that the term 'lexical item' is used in preference to 'word', 'word' being reserved as the name for a grammatical unit, that unit whose exponents, more than those of any other unit, are lexical items. (1961, 273)

405 The task of lexis can be summed up, by illustration, as that it has to account for the likelihood of 'wingless green insects' and for the, by contrast, unlikelihood of 'colourless green ideas'. (1961, 275)

406 It seems that two fundamental categories are needed /in lexis/, which we may call 'collocation' and 'set'. (1961, 276)

407 Collocation is the syntagmatic association of lexical items, quantifiable, textually, as the probability that there will occur, at n removes (a distance of n lexical items) from an item x, the items a, b, c . . . Any given item thus enters into a range of collocation, the items with which it is collocated being ranged from more to less probable . . . (1961, 276)

408 Items can . . . be grouped together by range of collocation, according to their overlap of, so to speak, collocational spread. The paradigmatic grouping which is thereby arrived at is the 'set'. (1961, 276)

409 In lexis, as in grammar, it is essential to distinguish between formal and contextual meaning. Once the formal description has identified the categories and the items, these can and must be treated contextually. (1961, 276)

410 In lexis as in grammar, the items have a contextual and a formal meaning: the definition aims at relating the lexical item, which is a linguistic item, to extralinguistic phenomena. For this it is necessary to use other words . . .
On the other hand, the citations are purely formal: they describe a word in relation to its linguistic environment. This relation between one word (or rather 'lexical item', since a lexical item is

often more than one grammatical word . . .) and another with which it is associated is called *collocation*. The collocation of words is the basic formal relation in lexis. (1961/66, 19)

411 Contextually, the /lexical/ set is a grouping of words having the same contextual range, functioning in the same situation types. (1961/66, 20)

412 . . . there may be one or more lexical items which are always tied to a particular grammatical structure; for example, the French expressions *le cas échéant* or *en (avoir) plein le dos*, or the English *let the cat out of the bag*. You cannot say *le cas échoit, est échu* or *the cat is in the bag*. This category may be called 'idioms'. (1961/66, 22)

413 We have distinguished lexis from grammar: not that there is no relation between them—on the contrary they are very closely linked—but because they involve different items and relations and consequently different methods and categories of description. (1961/66, 22)

414 Lexical power is the measure of the restriction on high probability collocation: the fewer the items with which a given item is likely to collocate (put another way, the more strongly the given item tends to be associated with certain other items), the more 'powerful' it is said to be. (1964a, 61)

415 . . . there is no rank scale in lexis . . . Lexical items are not organized by rank. (1964b, 34)

416 In lexis, not only are there more items to choose from at any given point, compared with the items or classes one is choosing from in grammar; also there is no line to be drawn between those that can and those that cannot be chosen. There are only 'more probable' and 'less probable' items. (1964b, 34)

417 The lexical item must be identified within lexis, on the basis of collocation. (1964b, 35)

418 Lexis has no category analogous to the grammatical 'unit', since there is no interrelated set of units (no rank scale) in lexis, but only the lexical item . . . (1964b, 35)

419 . . . the relation between the two levels /grammar and lexis/ is . . . a 'cline': formal patterns in all languages shade gradually from the grammatical to the lexical. (1964b, 35)

420 . . . language is a unified activity in which all patterning is subject to succession in time: there are thus analogies between the categories of lexis and those of grammar, analogies based on the two fundamental dimensions of any patterned activity, chain (one thing after another) and choice (one thing as opposed to another). (1964b, 35)

421 The lexical set is identified by privilege of occurrence in collocation, just as the grammatical class is identified by privilege of occurrence in structure; the set, in other words, is a grouping of items with similar tendencies of collocation. (1964/67, 220)

422 Lexical cohesion in its clearest form is provided by two or more occurrences, in close proximity, of the same lexical item; less strongly by the co-occurrence of items paradigmatically related in the sense that they may belong to the same lexical set. (1964/67, 220)

423 . . . lexis may be usefully thought of (a) as within linguistic form, and thus standing in the same relation to (lexical) semantics as does grammar to (grammatical) semantics, and (b) as not within grammar, lexical patterns thus being treated as different in kind, and not merely in delicacy, from grammatical patterns. This view is perhaps implicit in Firth's recognition of a 'collocational level'. (1966c, 148)

424 Lexical statements, or 'rules', need not be statistical, or even corpus-based, provided that their range of validity is defined in some other way, as by the introduction of a category of 'lexicalness' to parallel that of grammaticalness. (1966c, 150)

425 . . . lexis seems to require the recognition merely of linear co-occurrence together with some measure of significant proximity, either a scale or at least a cut-off point. It is this syntagmatic relation which is referred to as 'collocation'. (1966c, 152)

426 If . . . one speaks of a lexical level, there is no question of asserting the 'independence' of such a level, whatever this might mean; what is implied is the internal consistency of the statements and their referability to a stated model. (1966c, 152)

427 Collocation and lexical set are mutually defining as are structure and system: the set is the grouping of members with like privilege of occurrence in collocation. (1966c, 153)

428 . . . in lexis we are concerned with a very simple set of relations into which enter a large number of items, which must therefore be differentiated qua items, whereas in grammar we are concerned with very complex and variable relations in which the primary differentiation is among the relations themselves . . . (1966c, 153)

429 . . . the lexical item is not necessarily coextensive on either /the syntagmatic or paradigmatic/ axis with the item, or rather with any of the items, identified and accounted for in the grammar. (1966c, 153)

430 . . . the lexical component requires not, as it were, a second 'runthrough' of the model designed for the grammar but rather a specifically lexical model with distinct, though analogous, categories and forms of statement. (1966c, 154)

431 It is the similarity of their collocational restriction which enables us to consider grouping lexical items into lexical sets. (1966c, 156)

432 The criterion for the definition of the lexical set is . . . the syntactic (downward) criterion of potentiality of occurrence. (1966c, 156)

433 . . . while grammatical structures are hierarchically ordered, . . . it does not seem useful to postulate such an ordered hierarchy for lexis. (1966c, 156)

434 . . . the only 'structural' relation in lexis is one of simple co-occurrence . . . (1966c, 157)

435 . . . the 'lexical series' . . . like its analogue in grammar, may or may not coincide with the syntactic grouping recognized as a 'set' . . . (1966c, 157)

436 . . . the criterion for the assignment of items to sets is collocational, this means to say that items showing a certain degree of likeness in their collocational patterning are assigned to the same set. This 'likeness' may be thought of in the following terms. If we consider n occurrences of a given (potential) item, calling this item the 'node', and examine its 'collocates' up to m places on either side, giving a 'span' of $2m$, the $2mn$ occurrences of collocates will show a certain frequency of distribution. (1966c, 158)

437 . . . lexis is more item-bound than grammar. (1966c, 158)

438 The occurrence of an item in a collocational environment can only be discussed in terms of probability; and, although cut-off points will need to be determined for the purpose of presenting the results, the interest lies in the degree of 'lexicalness' of different collocations (of items and of sets), all of which are clearly regarded as 'lexical'. (1966c, 159)

439 A thesaurus of English based on formal criteria, giving collocationally defined lexical sets with citations to indicate the defining environments, would be a valuable complement to Roget's brilliant work of intuitive semantic classification in which lexical items are arranged 'according to the *ideas* which they express'. (1966c, 160)

440 . . . one cannot really separate vocabulary from grammar; the two form a single component in the linguistic system . . . (1973b, xi)

441 . . . the lexical density of a text . . . means the proportion of lexical items (content words) to words as a whole . . . (1974a, 32)

442 The lexical system is not something that is slotted in afterwards to a set of slots defined by the grammar. The lexicon—if I may go back to a definition I used many years ago—is simply the most delicate grammar. In other words, there is only one network of lexicogrammatical options. (1974b, 90)

443 . . . the need for the lexicogrammatical level of coding intermediate between meaning and sound arises not merely because of the increased semantic load that the system has to bear, but also because there has to be a means of mapping on to one another meanings deriving from different origins. This is achieved by grammatical structure. (1975c, 30)

444 The popular term 'wording' refers to lexicogrammatical form, the choice of words and grammatical structures. Within this stratum, there is no hard-and-fast division between vocabulary and grammar; the guiding principle in language is that the more general meanings are expressed through the grammar, and the more specific meanings through the vocabulary. (1976b, 5)

445 Lexical cohesion . . . regularly leaps over a number of sentences to pick up an element that has not figured in the intervening text . . . (1976b, 16)

446 . . . a lexical item (member of an open set) . . . (1976b, 274)

447 . . . lexical cohesion. This is the cohesive effect achieved by the selection of vocabulary. (1976b, 274)

448 The concept of the lexical item . . . is not totally clearcut; like most linguistic categories, although clearly defined in the ideal, it presents many indeterminacies in application to actual instances. Despite this indeterminacy—and it may be remarked that the term LEXICAL ITEM is rather less indeterminate than the folk-linguistic term WORD—it is an essential concept for the understanding of text. (1976b, 292)

449 Lexical cohesion is, as its name implies, lexical; it involves a kind of choice that is open-ended, the selection of a lexical item that is in some way related to one occurring previously. (1976b, 303)

450 Lexicogrammatical $\begin{cases} \text{Grammatical} \\ \text{Lexical} \end{cases}$ (1976b, 318)

451 Lexical cohesion embraces two distinct though related aspects which we referred to as REITERATION and COLLOCATION. (1976b, 318)

452 The whole of the vocabulary of a language is internally structured and organized along many dimensions, which collectively determine 'what goes with what'; these tendencies are as much a part of the linguistic system as are the principles of grammatical structure, even though they are statable only as tendencies, not as 'rules'. (1976b, 320)

453 It is the essentially probabilistic nature of lexical patterning which makes it so effective in the creation of texture . . . (1976b, 320)

5
Idealization

454   The originality of a person's use of his language consists in his selecting a feature not where it is impossible (has nct been previously selected) but where another would be more probable—and even more in his balanced combination of the improbable with the probable . . . (1964a, 66–7)

455   . . . linguistic competence is not the only aspect of language that deserves serious study: the explanation of linguistic performance can also be regarded as a reasonable goal and one that is still, as it were, internal to linguistics. (1964c, 191)

456   If I were to characterize the work in which I have been engaged together with some of my colleagues, I would say that our aim is to show the patterns inherent in the linguistic performance of the native speaker: this is what we mean by 'how the language works'. (1964c, 193)

457   Let us distinguish . . . between two components of knowing one's language: the knowledge of the language systems, and the knowledge of the uses of the system. (1968b, 96)

458   Here we shall not need to draw a distinction between an idealized knowledge of a language and its actualized use: between 'the code' and 'the use of the code', or between 'competence' and 'performance'. Such a dichotomy runs the risk of being either unnecessary or misleading: unnecessary if it is just another name for the distinction between what we have been able to describe in the grammar and what we have not, and misleading in any other interpretation. (1970b, 145)

459 A word or two should be said here about the relation of the concept of meaning potential to the Chomskyan notion of competence, even if only very briefly. The two are somewhat different. Meaning potential is defined not in terms of the mind but in terms of the culture; not as what the speaker knows, but as what he can do—in the special sense of what he can do linguistically (what he 'can mean', as we have expressed it). The distinction is important because 'can do' is of the same order of abstraction as 'does'; the two are related simply as potential to actualized potential, and can be used to illuminate each other. But 'knows' is distinct and clearly insulated from 'does'; the relation between the two is complex and oblique, and leads to the quest for a 'theory of performance' to explain the 'does'. (1971a, 52, 53)

460 There is always some idealization, where linguistic generalizations are made, but in a sociological context this has to be, on the whole, at a much lower level. We have, in fact, to 'come closer to what is actually said'; partly because the solutions to problems may depend on studying what is actually said, but also because even when this is not the case the features that are behaviourally relevant may be just those that the idealizing process most readily irons out. (1971a, 54)

461 If we insist on drawing a boundary between what /the speaker/ does and what he knows, we cannot explain what he does; what he does will appear merely as a random selection from within what he knows. But in the study of language in a social perspective we need both to pay attention to what is said and at the same time to relate it systematically to what might have been said but was not. Hence we do not make a dichotomy between knowing and doing; instead we place 'does' in the environment of 'can do', and treat language as speech potential. (1971a, 67)

462 The image of language as having a 'pure' form (*langue*) that becomes contaminated in the process of being translated into speech (*parole*) is of little value in a sociological context. We do not want a boundary between language and speech at all, or between pairs such as langue and parole, or competence and performance—unless these are reduced to mere synonyms of 'can do' and 'does'. (1971a, 67)

463 We are likely to find ourselves entangled in this problem, or trying to force a distinction between meaning and function, if we insist on characterizing language subjectively as the ability, or competence, of the speaker, instead of objectively as a potential, a set of alternatives. Hence my preference for the concept of 'meaning potential', which is what the speaker/hearer *can* (what he can mean, if you like), not what he knows. The two are, to an extent, different ways of looking at the same thing; but the former, 'inter-organism' perspective has different implications from the latter, 'intra-organism' one. (1973a, 25)

464 There is no sense in which we can maintain that /the child/ knows a linguistic form but cannot use it. (1973b, xii)

465 . . . the intraorganism perspective, language as knowledge, and the interorganism perspective, language as behaviour. These both lead us outward from language as a system, the former into the region of psychological studies, the latter into sociology and related fields. (1974a, 7)

466 We do not simply 'know' our mother tongue as an abstract system of vocal signals, or as if it was some sort of a grammar book with a dictionary attached. We know it in the sense of knowing how to use it; we know how to communicate with other people, how to choose forms of language that are appropriate to the type of situation we find ourselves in, and so on. All this can be expressed as 'know how to'; as a form of knowledge: we know how to behave linguistically. (1974a, 9)

467 . . . there is no difference between knowing language and knowing how to use it . . . (1974a, 55–6)

468 . . . these two perspectives—on the one hand the intra-organism perspective, language as what goes on inside the head (language as knowledge), and on the other hand the inter-organism perspective, language as what goes on between people (language as interaction, or simply as behaviour)—are complementary and not contradictory. (1974b, 81)

469 . . . once you become concerned with the linguistic system as a whole, including the semantic system, then you have to look outside language for your criteria of *idealization*. (1974b, 82)

470 If you are interested in linguistic *inter-action*, you don't want the high level of idealization that is involved in the notion of competence; you can't use it, because most of the distinctions that are important to you are idealized out of the picture. (1974b, 84, 85)

471 . . . we don't try to draw a distinction between what is grammatical and what is acceptable. So in an inter-organism perspective there is no place for the dichotomy of competence and performance, opposing what the speaker knows to what he does. There is no need to bring in the question of what the speaker knows; the background to what he does is what he could do—a potential, which is objective, not a competence, which is subjective. (1974b, 85)

472 There will always be *idealization* in any study of language, or indeed in any systematic inquiry. The point is here that we need to reduce the level of idealization, to make it as low as possible . . . We have to impose as low a degree of idealization on the facts as is compatible with a systematic inquiry. This means, in other words, that what is grammatical is defined as what is acceptable. There is no distinction between these two, from which it follows that there is no place for a distinction between competence and performance or between *langue* and *parole*, because the only distinction that remains is that between the *actual*, and the *potential* of which it is an actualization. (1974b, 99)

473 . . . there are two main perspectives on language: one is the intra-organism perspective, the other is the inter-organism perspective. In the intra-organism perspective we see language as what goes on in the head; in the inter-organism perspective it is what goes on between two people. Now these two perspectives are complementary, and in my opinion linguistics is in the most healthy state when both are taken seriously. (1974b, 112)

474 Creativity does not consist in creating new sentences. Creativity consists in new interpretations of existing behaviour in existing social contexts; in new semiotic patterns, however realized . . . I think the creativity of the individual is a function of the social system. (1974b, 117)

6
Language & Culture

475 . . . there is nothing in the nature of our general experience that would make us treat social roles and social relationships grammatically like concrete objects, and some languages do not. It is our language that structures our experience for us in this particular way. (1968b, 100)

476 Our experience is in fact organized on many levels at once, and we abstract from it a whole lot of different layers of generalization; we are not by any means shackled by the structure imposed by our language system. But the language system is the principal agency for our conceptualization . . . (1968b, 100–101)

477 A significant fact about the behaviour of human beings in relation to their social environment is that a large part of it is linguistic behaviour. The study of social man presupposes the study of language and social man. (1971a, 48)

478 The study of language as social behaviour is in the last resort an account of semantic options deriving from the social structure. (1971a, 64)

479 . . . the total range of meanings that is embodied in and realized through the language system is determined by the context of the culture—in other words by the social structure. (1971a, 64)

480 The concept of socio-linguistics ultimately implies a 'socio-semantics' which is a genuine meeting ground of two ideologies, the social and the linguistic. And this faces both ways. The options in meaning are significant linguistically because selections in grammar and vocabulary can be explained as a realization of them. They are significant sociologically because they provide insight into patterns of behaviour that are in turn explainable as realizations of the pragmatic and symbolic acts that are the expressions of the social structure. (1971a, 64–5)

481 To understand language, we examine the way in which the social structure is realized through language: how values are transmitted, roles defined and behaviour patterns made manifest. (1971a, 69)

482 The social functions of language clearly determine the pattern of language varieties, or 'registers'; the register range, or linguistic repertoire, of a community or of an individual is derived from the range of uses that language is put to in that particular culture or sub-culture. (1973a, 22)

483 When we talk of 'social functions of language', we mean those contexts which are significant in that we are able to specify some of the meaning potential that is characteristically, and explainably, associated with them. And we shall be particularly interested if we find that in doing so we can throw light on certain features in the internal organization of language. (1973a, 26–7)

484 How else can one look at language *except* in a social context? (1974a, 5)

485 We can think of any social institution, from the linguistic point of view, as a communication network . . . The structure of the institution will be enshrined in the language, in the different types of interaction that take place and the linguistic registers associated with them. (1974a, 58)

486 . . . those wanting to talk about language from the point of view not so much that 'people talk' but that 'people talk to each other' have called what they are doing sociolinguistics. I think both

Hymes and Labov have pointed out that the 'socio' is really unnecessary, and I agree with them. (1974b, 81)

487 The culture is itself a semiotic system, a system of meanings or information that is encoded in the behaviour potential of the members, including their verbal potential—that is, their linguistic system. The linguistic system is only one form of the realization of the more general semiotic system which constitutes the culture. (1975c, 36)

488 We /take/ the view of the social system as a semiotic, a system of meanings that is *realized through* (inter alia) the linguistic system. The linguistic semiotic—that is, semantics—is one form of the realization of the social semiotic. (1975c, 121)

489 The social semiotic is the system of meanings that defines or constitutes the culture; and the linguistic system is one mode of realization of these meanings. (1975c, 139)

490 We are not the prisoners of our cultural semiotic; we can all learn to move outside it. But this requires a positive act of semiotic reconstruction. We are socialized within it, and our meaning potential is derived from it. (1975c, 140)

7
Language Learning

---

491 . . . the most significant fact about the child's learning of his native language is that he has no language through which to learn it. (1968b, 95)

492 One acquires the language system through mastering its use, and one extends its use by acquiring more of the system; the two go together in general, in the language learning process. (1968b, 96)

493 The child's understanding of what language is is derived from his own experience of language in situations of use. It thus embodies all of the images we have described: the instrumental, the regulatory, the interactional, the personal, the heuristic, the imaginative and the representational. Each of these is his interpretation of a function of language with which he is familiar. (1969b, 17)

494 The child's awareness of language cannot be isolated from his awareness of language function . . . (1969b, 20)

495 . . . the adult model provides /the child/ with instances which are from his point of view not nearly as fragmentary and disordered as we are sometimes invited to think. (1970c, 323)

496 The phenomena of linguistic ontogeny are . . . functionally complex: the child's developing language system represents a progressive adjustment between structures derived from his own uses of language, that is, from those functions which he has already acquired, and the structures of the model to which he has access—structures which are themselves functional in origin. (1970c, 323)

497 . . . learning the mother tongue is, in effect, learning the functions of language, which in turn provide the content for and give significance to its structures and systems. (1970c, 360)

498 Learning one's mother tongue is learning the uses of language, and the meanings, or rather the meaning potential, associated with them. The structures, the words and the sounds are the realization of this meaning potential. Learning language is learning how to mean. (1973a, 24)

499 The language system of the very young child is, effectively, a set of restricted language varieties; and it is characteristic of young children's language that its internal form reflects rather directly the function that it is being used to serve. What the child does with language tends to determine its structure. (1973a, 27)

500 . . . it is through the gradual extension of his meaning potential into new functions that the child's linguistic horizons become enlarged. (1973a, 33)

501 What happens in the course of maturation is a process that we might from one point of view call 'functional reduction', whereby the original functional range of the child's language—a set of fairly discrete functional components each with its own meaning potential—is gradually replaced by a more highly coded and more abstract, but also simpler, functional system. (1973a, 36)

502 Looking at the early stages of language development from a functional viewpoint, we can follow the process whereby the child gradually 'learns how to mean'—for this is what first-language learning is. (1974a, 16)

503 In order for language to be a means of learning, it is essential for the child to be able to encode in language, through words and structures, his experience of processes of the external world and of the people and things that participate in them. (1974a, 18)

504 The child learns his mother tongue in the context of behavioural settings where the norms of the culture are acted out and enunciated for him, settings of parental control, instruction, personal interaction, and the like; and, reciprocally, he is 'socialized' into the value systems and behaviour patterns of the culture through the use of language at the same time as he is learning it. (1974a, 21)

505 Learning language consists in part in learning to free it from the constraints of the immediate environment. (1974a, 29)

506 . . . the very young child, in his first ventures with language, keeps the functions of language fairly clearly apart; when he speaks, he is doing only one thing at a time . . . (1974a, 31)

507 . . . a child who is learning language is learning 'how to mean'; that is, he is developing a semantic potential, in respect of a set of functions in language that are in the last resort social functions. (1974b, 110)

508 There has been a myth around over the past few years that the child must have a specific innate language-learning capacity, a built-in grammar, because the data to which he is exposed are insufficient to account for the result. Now that is not true. The language around him is fantastically rich and highly structured; Labov has said this and he is quite right. It is quite unnecessary to postulate a learning device having these highly specific linguistic properties. That doesn't mean it is wrong; it means it isn't necessary. (1974b, 110)

509 Early language development may be interpreted as the child's progressive mastery of a functional potential. (1975c, 5)

510 . . . the learning of language will be interpreted as the learning of a system of meanings. (1975c, 8)

511 A child who is learning his first language is learning how to mean;

in this perspective, the linguistic system is to be seen as a semantic potential. It is a range of possible meanings; together with the means whereby these meanings are realized, or expressed. (1975c, 8)

512 . . . the learning of language is essentially the learning of a semantic system, and . . . this process is already well under way before the child has any words at all. He learns to mean long before he adopts the lexical mode for the realization of meanings. (1975c, 9)

513 . . . in the developmental process language is the primary /symbolic system/. A child's construction of a semantic system and his construction of a social system take place side by side, as two aspects of a single unitary process. (1975c, 121)

514 In principle, a child is learning one semiotic system, the culture, and simultaneously he is learning the means of learning it—a second semiotic system, the language, which is the intermediary in which the first one is encoded. (1975c, 122)

515 The child's task is to construct the system of meanings that represents his own model of social reality. This process takes place inside his own head; it is a cognitive process. But it takes place in contexts of social interaction, and there is no way it can take place except in these contexts. (1975c, 139)

516 As well as being a cognitive process, the learning of the mother tongue is also an interactive process. It takes the form of the continued exchange of meanings between the self and others. (1975c, 139-40)

517 The social context is . . . not so much an external condition on the learning of meanings as a generator of the meanings that are learnt. And part of the social context is the language that is used by the interactants—the language the child hears around him. (1975c, 140)

518 The essential condition of learning is the systematic link between semantic categories and the semiotic properties of the situation. The child can learn to mean because the linguistic features in some sense relate to features of the environment. But the environment is a social construct. It does not consist of things, or even of processes and relations; it consists of human interaction, from which the things derive their meaning. (1975c, 140–41)

519 It is clear that the awareness of text that we develop as part of the learning of the mother tongue is rather free from constraints of time, and depends much more on contextual relevance and integration of the language with the environment. (1976b, 296)

8
Levels

---

520 The primary levels are 'form', 'substance', and 'context'. (1961, 243)

521 The theory requires that linguistic events should be accounted for at a number of different levels: this is found to be necessary because of the difference in kind of the processes of abstraction involved. (1961, 243)

522 The complete framework of levels requires certain further subdivisions and additions, and is as follows:
(a) Substance may be either 'phonic' or 'graphic'
(b) If substance is phonic, it is related to form by 'phonology'
(c) If substance is graphic, it is related to form by 'orthography' (or, 'graphology'), either
    (i) if the script is lexical, then directly, or
    (ii) if the script is phonological, then via phonology
(d) Form is in fact two related levels, 'grammar' and 'lexis'
(e) Context is in fact (like phonology) an 'interlevel', relating form to extratextual features. (1961, 244)

523 . . . in theory and in description it is essential to separate the levels first and then relate them. The theoretical reason is that different *kinds* of abstraction are involved, and therefore different categories. In description, the attempt to account for the data at all levels at once results in a failure to account for them fully at any level. If one rejects the separation of levels and wishes, for example, to combine grammatical and phonological criteria to yield a single set of units, the description becomes intolerably complex. (1961, 268)

524 . . . it is misleading to think of the levels as forming a hierarchy. They represent different aspects of the 'patternness' of linguistic activity. (1961, 269)

525 Though there is no precedence or priority, there is of course order among the levels, as determined by their specific interrelations; in the study of language as a whole form is pivotal, since it is through grammar and lexis that language activity is—and is shown to be—meaningful. (1961, 269)

526 . . . phonology is an 'interlevel' . . . (1961, 269)

527 The levels of analysis are derived in the first place by a process of abstraction from our observations of the language material. (1961/66, 5)

528 These . . . are what we call the 'levels of analysis' of descriptive linguistics: phonic, phonological, grammatical, lexical and contextual. (1961/66, 5)

529 . . . the usefulness of linguistic theory in application to literary studies depends on its ability both to comprehend and to integrate all the levels of language. (1964a, 67)

530 . . . not only must the literary analyst have access to theories for the description of all levels of linguistic patterning—grammar, lexis, phonology and phonetics, and their graphic parallels—but he must be able to see them in interaction as they must always interact in any language event. (1964a, 67)

531 It should not be forgotten that the description of a language forms a unified whole. We have to separate the different levels, in order to say anything useful at all; not only in the analysis, but also in the presentation, when the description is 'written up' as it were. But this separation is never rigid or opaque. . . . In presentation, the levels, first separated, are brought into relation with each other . . . We are describing language as used by human beings, and they do not use just one level of it at a time. (1964b, 47)

532 . . . there are two different levels of language whose items can be represented by the symbols of a script. One is form, the other phonology, the symbols either stand for the *formal* items, grammatical and lexical, of the language, or they stand for *phonological* items. (1964b, 48)

533 The 'graphological' level of language, whatever the nature of the script, is characterized by its own distinctive patterns . . . (1964b, 51)

534 If we admit that there is a *semantic* system, a semantic level of organization within the linguistic system, then the question we are asking is 'What is above that?'; and it is at that point that we move outside language. We are regarding semantics as an interface between language and something else, and it is to that something else that we go for our criteria of idealization. (1974b, 82)

535 The semantic level in the linguistic system is, among other things, an interface between language and the realities of the outside world. (1976b, 305)

9
Meaning

9.1 Meaning

536 The term 'meaning' will not be used; Meaning is regarded as a function of the description at all levels, so that reference to context in a grammatical statement implies the establishment of relations between grammatical and contextual meaning. (1956a, 179)

537 A descriptive grammar of the language of a given text deals with 'the meaning of the whole event'; the meaning is not separate from or opposed to the linguistic form but is a function of the whole text. The complete text has meaning in the social context in which it operates, and this is to be stated by the procedure of 'contextualization'. (1959, 9–10)

538 'Meaning' is a concept, and a technical term, of the theory. (1961, 243)

539 Contextual meaning, which is an extension of the popular—and traditional linguistic—notion of meaning, is quite distinct from formal meaning and has nothing whatever to do with 'information'. The contextual meaning of an item is its relation to extratextual features; but this is not a direct relation of the item as such, but of the item in its place in linguistic form: contextual meaning is therefore logically dependent on formal meaning. (1961, 245)

540 But 'meaning' in linguistics has to be used in a broader way, to cover not only CONTEXTUAL MEANING but also FORMAL MEANING. The reason is that if we want to understand how language works we must realize that form, the purely internal patterning of language, is also meaningful. (1964b, 37–8)

541 The term 'meaning' in its lay use usually suggests experiential, or experiential together with logical, meaning; but if the implication is that other areas of syntactic choice are not meaningful it may be desirable to emancipate technical usage from everyday terminology in this respect. (1968a, 209)

542 Meaning is at the same time both a component of social action and a symbolic representation of the structure of social action. The semiotic structure of the environment—the ongoing social activity, the roles and the statuses, and the interactional channels—both determines the meanings exchanged and is created by and formed out of them. (1975c, 143)

9.2 Meaning Potential

543 . . . when we examine the meaning potential of language itself, we find that the vast numbers of options embodied in it combine into a very few relatively independent 'networks'; and these networks of options correspond to certain basic functions of language. This enables us to give an account of the different functions of language that is relevant to the general understanding of linguistic structure rather than to any particular psychological or sociological investigation. (1970b, 142)

544 The potential of language is a meaning potential. This meaning potential is the linguistic realization of the behaviour potential; 'can mean' is 'can do' when translated into language. The meaning potential is in turn realized in the language system as lexicogrammatical potential, which is what the speaker 'can say'. (1971a, 51)

545 The meaning potential is the range of *significant* variation that is at the disposal of the speaker. (1971a, 54)

546 The investigation of language as social behaviour is not only relevant to the understanding of social structure; it is also relevant to the understanding of language. A network of socio-semantic options—the representation of what we have been calling the 'meaning potential'—has implications in both directions; on the one hand as the realization of patterns of behaviour and, on the other hand, as realized by the patterns of grammar. The concept of meaning potential thus provides a perspective on the nature of language. Language is as it is because of its function in the social structure, and the organization of behavioural meanings should give some insight into its social foundations. (1971a, 65)

547 . . . our functional picture of the adult linguistic system is of a culturally specific and situationally sensitive range of meaning potential. (1974a, 35)

548 The meaning potential is what can be meant—the potential of the semantic system. (1975c, 124)

9.3 Semantics

549 Semantics . . . is 'what the speaker can mean'. It is the strategy that is available for entering the language system. It is one form of, or rather one form of the realization of, behaviour potential; 'can mean' is one form of 'can do'. The behaviour potential may be realized not only by language but also by other means. Behavioural strategies are outside language but may be actualized through the medium of the language system. (1972a, 72)

550 . . . the semantic options are relatable to recognizable features in the grammar, even though the relationship will often be a rather complex one. (1972a, 75)

551 . . . the semantic network is an account of how social meanings are expressed in language. It is the linguistic realization of patterns of behaviour. (1972a, 79)

552 The input to the semantic networks is sociological and specific; their output is linguistic and general. (1972a, 80)

553 We cannot, as a rule, relate behavioural options directly to the grammar. The relationship is too complex, and some intermediate level of representation is needed through which we express the meaning potential that is associated with the particular behavioural context. It is this intermediate level that constitutes our 'sociological' semantics. The semantic network then takes us, by a second step, into the linguistic patterns that can be recognized and stated in grammatical terms. (1972a, 83)

554 These /semantic/ networks are what we understand by 'semantics'. They constitute a stratum that is intermediate between the social system and the grammatical system. The former is wholly outside language, the latter is wholly within language; the semantic networks, which describe the range of alternative meanings available to the speaker in given social contexts and settings, form a bridge between the two. (1972a, 96)

555 What the speaker can say, i.e., the lexicogrammatical system as a whole, operates as the realization of the semantic system, which is what the speaker *can mean*—what I refer to as the 'meaning potential'. I see language essentially as a system of meaning potential. Now, once we go outside language, then we see that this semantic system is itself the realization of something beyond, which is what the speaker can do—I have referred to that as the 'behaviour potential'. (1974b, 86)

556 Each level is a network of paradigmatic relations, of OR's—a range of alternatives, in the sociological sense. This is what I mean by a *potential*: the semantic system is a network of meaning potential. The network consists very simply of a set of interrelated systems . . . (1974b, 87)

557 The term semantic is not to be understood in the restricted sense of 'lexicosemantic', i.e., concerned with the meanings of words. It refers to the totality of meaning in language, whether such meaning is encoded in the form of vocabulary or not. (1975c, 9)

558 The semantic system evolved, we assume, operationally, as a form of symbolic interaction in social contexts; so there is every reason that it should reflect the structure of such contexts in its own internal organization. (1975c, 131–2)

10
Nature of Language

559 Language has 'formal meaning' and 'contextual meaning'. (1961, 244)

560 Language is patterned activity. (1961, 250)

561 Our predecessors thought of language as an organism, and drew their analogies from evolution. We reject this as misleading; but no less misleading is its familiar substitute, according to which language is an edifice and the morphemes are the bricks. Perhaps if language had been thought of as activity we should never have heard of 'morphemics'. (1961, 279n)

562 If language is a code, where is the pre-coded message? (1961, 280n)

563 Language . . . can be thought of as *organized* noise. To this we can add: 'used in situations', actual social situations. Organized noise used in social situations, or in other words, 'contextualized systematic sounds'. (1961/66, 3)

564 . . . language is meaningful activity. (1961/66, 4)

565 . . . language is best regarded as a form of activity. Specifically, it is a form of activity of human beings in societies; and it has the property of being patterned. (1964b, 4)

566 Language does not exist: it happens. It is neither an organism, as many nineteenth-century linguistics saw it, nor an edifice, as it was regarded in the early modern 'structuralist' period of linguistics. Language is activity . . . (1964b, 9)

567 Essentially, any language is as good as any other language, in the sense that every language is equally well adapted to the uses to which the community puts it. There is no such thing as a 'primitive' language. (1964b, 99)

568 Language is a form of culturally determined behaviour and this behaviour includes the ability to take on a range of linguistically defined roles in speech situations. (1968b, 98)

569 The child knows what language is because he knows what language does. (1969b, 10)

570 The nature of language is closely related to the demands that we make on it, the functions it has to serve. (1970b, 141)

571 Considering language in its social context . . . we can describe it in broad terms as a behaviour potential; and more specifically as a meaning potential, where meaning is a form of behaving . . . (1971a, 55)

572 We shall define language as 'meaning potential': that is, as sets of options, or alternatives, in meaning, that are available to the speaker-hearer. (1972a, 72)

573 In the evolution of language as a whole, the form of language has been determined by the functions it has to serve. (1972a, 100)

574 The internal organization of natural language can best be explained in the light of the social functions which language has evolved to serve. Language is as it is because of what it has to do. (1973a, 34)

575 Language is being regarded as the encoding of a 'behaviour potential' into a 'meaning potential'; that is, as a means of expressing what the human organism 'can do', in interaction with other human organisms, by turning it into what he 'can mean'. (1974a, 19)

576 There is no *a priori* reason why human language should have taken just the evolutionary path that it has taken and no other; our brains could have produced a symbolic system of quite a different kind. (1974a, 19)

577 Language . . . is a potential: it is what the speaker can do. What a person can do in the linguistic sense, that is, what he can do as speaker/hearer, is equivalent to what he 'can mean': hence the description of language as a 'meaning potential'. (1974a, 27)

578 . . . all speech other than the protolanguage of infancy is polyphonic: different melodies are kept going side by side, and each element in the sentence is like a chord which contributes something to all of them. This is perhaps the most striking characteristic of human language, and one which distinguishes it from all other symbolic communication systems. (1974a, 31)

579 . . . all language is language-in-use, in a context of situation, and all of it relates to the situation . . . (1974a, 34)

580 Language is the ability to 'mean' in the situation types, or social contexts, that are generated by the culture. (1974a, 35)

581 . . . I see language as a *meaning* potential. It is a form of *human semiotic*, in fact the main form of human semiotic, and as such I want to characterize it in terms of the part it plays in the life of social man. (1974b, 98).

582 Language expresses both human biology and human culture. It expresses the unity of the human race and it expresses the diversity of human culture. Experience is a product of both, and experience is encoded in language; but it is experience as processed by the culture and by the sub-culture. (1974b, 118)

583 We cannot give anything approaching a definitive answer to the question why the human semiotic should have taken precisely this form and no other; but we can begin to look into it: and for this purpose we need a theory of linguistic functions. (1974c, 45)

584 In principle, language is as it is because of the functions it has evolved to serve. (1974c, 45)

585 We take it for granted that language is a multiple coding system, organized into levels, or 'strata'. (1974c, 50)

11
Scales

11.1 Delicacy

586 Delicacy is distinct from rank and the limit of delicacy applies at the rank of all units . . . (1961, 272)

587 Delicacy is the scale of differentiation, or depth in detail. It is a cline, whose limit at one end is the primary degree in the categories of structure and class. In the theory, the other limit is the point beyond which no further grammatical relations obtain. (1961, 272)

588 Each subsequent increase in delicacy delays the move to the exponents and thus increases the grammaticalness of the description. (1961, 272)

589 At one stage, . . . /delicacy/ becomes a limit on the grammatical differentiation of items which then remain to be lexically differentiated: it sets an endpoint to grammar where lexis takes over. (1961, 272)

590 /When lexis takes over the grammar/ the scales of delicacy and exponence meet. The endpoint set to grammar on the exponence scale is where abstraction ceases: one has to move from abstract category to exponential item. That set on the delicacy scale is where differentiation ceases: the set of exponents of each class, and of each element of structure, permits no further, more delicate groupings. If the formal items are still not ranged in systems, the implication in either case is that further relations among them are lexical. (1961, 272–3)

591 It is worth insisting . . . that delicacy is a cline . . . (1961, 287)

592 Delicacy can be illustrated with reference either to structure or to system . . . (1964c, 194)

593 . . . the *scale of delicacy* . . ., besides being of theoretical interest in providing a measure of the status of a given contrast in the language and of the degree and kind of deviation of deviant utterances, has proved of value in textual analysis because it provides a variable cut-off point for description: the analyst can go as far as he wishes for his own purpose in depth of detail and then stop. (1964c, 194)

11.2 Depth

594 Depth is the degree of recursion attained in a recursive structure . . . (1966d, 180)

11.3 Exponence

595 'Manifestation' (in substance) and 'realization' (in form) are introduced here to represent different degrees along the scale of exponence . . . I have used 'exponent' as indicating *relative* position on the exponence scale (a formal item as exponent of a formal category, and a feature of substance as exponent of a formal category or item) . . . (1961, 250n)

596 . . . exponence is the *only* relation by which formal category, formal item and feature of substance are linked on a *single* scale: hence the need for a single term to indicate relative position on the scale. Two defined positions on this scale can then be distinguished as 'realization' and 'manifestation'. (1961, 250n)

597 Exponence is the scale which relates the categories of the theory, which are categories of the highest degree of abstraction, to the data. (1961, 270)

11.4 More/Less

598 . . . the 'more/less' relation itself, far from being an unexpected complication in grammar, is in fact a basic feature of language and is treated as such by the theory. It is not simply that all grammar can be stated in probability terms, based on frequency counts in texts: this is due to the nature of the text as a sample. But the very fact that we can recognize primary and secondary structures—that there is a scale of delicacy at all—shows that the nature of language is *not* to operate with relations of 'always this and never that'. Grammatical theory takes this into account by introducing a special scale, that of delicacy, to handle the improbability of certainty . . . (1961, 259)

599 . . . forms which lie on the borderline between two types and could be interpreted as one or the other. The situation is a familiar one in many fields, and when one is attempting to explain phenomena as complex as those of human language it would be surprising to find things otherwise. (1976b, 88)

11.5 Rank

600 The scale on which the units are in fact ranged in the theory needs a name, and may be called 'rank'. (1961, 251)

601 . . . the theory allows for downward 'rank shift': the transfer of a (formal realization of a) given unit to a lower rank. Second, it does not allow for upward shift. Third, only whole units can enter into higher units. (1961, 251)

602 . . . it seems worth while making use of 'syntax' and 'morphology' in the theory, to refer to direction on the rank scale. 'Syntax' is then the downward relation, 'morphology' the upward one; *and both go all the way.* (1961, 262)

603 In relating the categories to each other and to their exponents, the theory needs to operate with three scales of abstraction, the scales of rank, exponence, and delicacy. (1961, 268)

604 Rank is distinct from both exponence and from delicacy. A shift in one never by itself entails a shift in either of the others. (1961, 270)

605 Shunting, or moving up and down the rank scale, is a part of descriptive method imposed by the theory to show the relation among the different units: to permit a unified description with links, through all categories, all the way from morpheme to sentence. (1961, 286)

606 . . . the phenomenon known as *rankshift* (or *downgrading*). Here an item of one rank is as it were shifted down the scale of rank to form part of an item either of lower rank than itself or of equal rank to itself . . . (1961/66, 10)

607 'Rankshift' is in fact merely a name for that type of recursive structure which cuts across the scale of rank. That is to say: in non-rankshift structures, whether recursive or not, classes of each rank enter into a structure of the rank immediately above . . . In rankshift, this relation is broken and the classes enter into a structure of their own rank or even lower rank than themselves . . . (1963a, 13)

608 By rank grammar I mean one which specifies and labels a fixed number of layers in the hierarchy of constituents, such that any constituent, and any constitute, can be assigned to one or other of the specified layers, or RANKS. (1966b, 111)

609 /A rank grammar/ defines a point of origin for structures and systems, so that the assignment of any item to a given rank, as also the assignment of the structures and systems themselves, becomes an important step in generalization. To show that a system operates at a given rank is the first step in stating its relationship to other systems; likewise to assign an item to a given rank is the first step in stating the systematic and structural relations into which it may enter and those which it may embody within itself. (1966b, 112)

610   . . . embedding (rankshift) . . . (1976b, 223)

11.6 Realization

---

611   The grammar of the clause may be represented as a network of . . . options, to each of which is attached a realization statement showing the structural 'output' of that option. In some cases . . . the realization statement merely specifies the presence of a certain structural function; but in other cases it may have the effect of ordering one function with respect to another or to initial or final position in the syntagm. But it may also specify the conflation of two functions into a single element of structure . . . (1969a, 250)

612   The concept of realization has been familiar in linguistics for a long time, though it has been called by different names; in English, exponence, implementation, manifestation as well as realization. (1969/76a, 4)

613   To each of the options . . . such as indicative, imperative etc., we may append a realization statement showing the contribution made by the selection of that option to the structure of the sentence . . . These are thought of as statements of relationship rather than as rules. (1969/76a, 5-6)

614   . . . the systemic and the structural descriptions are related by realization statements which show the structural contribution of the options in the grammar. (1969/76a, 6)

615   . . . much of linguistic description consists in accounting for the fact that things are different and yet identical at the same time—the notion of realization expresses just that. (1970c, 347)

616   Grammar is what the speaker CAN SAY, and is the realization of what he MEANS. Semantics is what he CAN MEAN; and we are looking at this as the realization of what he DOES. But it is 'realization' in a somewhat different sense, because what he CAN DO lies outside language . . . (1972a, 82)

617 To my mind, the key concept is that of *realization*, language as multiple coding. Just as there is a relation of realization between the semantic system and the lexicogrammatical system, so that *can say* is the *realization* of *can mean*, so also there is a relation of realization between the semantic system and some higher-level semiotic which we can represent if you like as a behavioural system. It would be better to say that *can mean* is 'a realization of *can do*', or rather 'is one form of the realization of *can do*'. (1974b, 86)

11.7 Scale Types

---

618 I have used the terms 'hierarchy', 'taxonomy', and 'cline' as general scale-types. (1961, 248)

619 A hierarchy is taken to mean a system of terms related along a single dimension which must be one involving some form of logical precedence (such as inclusion). (1961, 248)

620 A taxonomy is taken to mean a special type of hierarchy, one with two additional characteristics: (i) there is a constant relation of each term to the term immediately following it, and a constant reciprocal relation of each to that immediately preceding it; and (ii) degree is significant, so that the place in order of each one of the terms, statable as the distance in number of steps from either end, is a defining characteristic of that term. (1961, 248–9)

621 A cline resembles a hierarchy in that it involves relation along a single dimension; but instead of being made up of a number of discrete terms a cline is a continuum carrying potentially infinite gradation. (1961, 249)

622 Immediate Constituent analysis, for example, yields a hierarchy that is not a taxonomy . . . (1961, 249n)

12
Subject

623 The structural element 'subject' in the present grammar is derived from the mood system, and thus corresponds more to the 'surface subject' of a transformational grammar. The concept of a 'deep subject' is unnecessary (and would be self-contradictory in this context) since the relations it is needed to account for are handled systematically. (1967b, 39n)

624 In clauses of all types, one 'participant' (that is, one participant role or combination of participant roles) is always expressed structurally in the subject. (1967b, 45)

625 The presence of an element 'subject' in the clause . . . is determined from outside the transitivity systems; the latter then assign to the subject a particular feature representing a participant role or role-combination from the set 'actor, initiator, goal, attributant'. (1967b, 45)

626 Treatment in terms of clause features enables us to generalize by saying that there are in fact three distinct types of subject, or subject functions, determined by the transitivity systems; these could be labelled 'ergative', 'nominative' and 'accusative' . . . (1967b, 46)

627 The subject is that nominal which, together with the finite verbal element, fulfils a modal role in the realization of speech function; the two together form a constituent specified by the mood systems . . . (1967c, 212)

628 The function 'subject' as understood here is specified in the mood systems, not in the transitivity systems; the term therefore corresponds to the 'surface subject' of a transformational grammar, not to the 'deep subject' (which is a transitivity function). (1967c, 212)

629 . . . the subject is that element which is introduced in the realization of certain features in the system network of mood. (1967c, 215)

630 In transitivity, the subject may be actor, goal, beneficiary or range. (1967c, 215)

631 In thematization, the subject may be (included within) theme or rheme . . . (1967c, 215)

632 In information focus, the subject may be (included within) given or new . . . (1967c, 215)

633 If the roles of actor and theme are combined . . . they are likely also to be combined with that of subject. (1967c, 216)

634 This distinction, between DIRECT and INDIRECT participants, is a structural one, but it is not irrelevant to the meaning: a direct participant can function as subject, whereas an indirect one cannot. (1969/76b, 160)

635 The choice of subject, for example, depends largely on thematic option since it is the participant functioning as theme rather than that functioning as actor that is normally chosen as the subject . . . (1969/76b, 169)

636 The location of the subject in the clause—before or after the finite element of the verb—is an expression of mood; and the reasons why the location of the subject expresses mood are thematic reasons. (1969/76b, 173)

637 Whether a particular element can be subject or not depends in principle on whether it is to be expressed as a direct or as an indirect participant (as a nominal or following a preposition), and this is primarily a question of transitivity . . . (1969/76b, 173)

638 The circumstantial functions seem less central to the process than do the participant functions; this is related to their inability to take on the role of subject. (1970b, 149)

639 The notion of subject conflates three distinct roles which, although they are typically combined into one element, are nevertheless independent of one another. (1970b, 159)

640 These three 'kinds of subject' relate to the functions of language . . . The logical subject is the actor; this is a transitivity role, deriving from the ideational function. The other two have different sources, though they are no less meaningful. The grammatical subject derives from the interpersonal component in language function; specifically, it has to do with the roles taken on by the performer and receiver in a communication situation. The psychological subject belongs to the textual component; it is concerned with the organization of the clause as a message, within a larger piece of discourse. (1970b, 159)

641 The function of the 'grammatical subject' is . . . a meaningful function in the clause, since it defines the communication role adopted by the speaker. (1970b, 160)

642 The notion 'grammatical subject' by itself is strange, since it implies a structural function whose only purpose is to define a structural function. Actually, just as the 'logical subject' is a function defined by transitivity, so the 'grammatical subject' is a function defined by mood. (1970b, 160)

643 . . . theme, actor and modal subject are identical unless there is good reason for them not to be. (1970b, 161)

644 The subject, in its traditional sense, is thus a complex of four distinct functions, three in the structure of the clause: 1. actor ('logical subject'): ideational; 2. modal subject ('grammatical subject'): interpersonal; 3. theme ('psychological subject'):

textual. Together with a fourth function which is in the structure of the 'information unit': 4. given ('psychological subject 2'): textual. These coincide unless there is 'good reason' for them not to do so . . . (1970b, 164–5)

645 The subject–predicate structure is entirely derivable from mood, and has no independent significance. (1970b, 165)

646 It is customary to recognize three 'types' of subject, the grammatical subject, the logical subject and the psychological subject; and although these terms are preposterous ('grammatical subject' suggests a structural element whose only function is to be a function in grammatical structure, and the other two are no better), the categories on the whole are clear enough . . . (1970c, 353)

647 . . . the subject in English is essential to the expression of mood; and in fact the organization of clauses into some form of predicative structure has in many languages a modal function, expressing the speaker's participation in, or intrusion into, the speech event: his choice of speech role (mood) and his assessment of the validity of what he is saying (modality). This in turn is part of a more general component of meaning which includes his attitudes and comments, assertions of familiarity and distance, and the like. (1974c, 47)

13
System

648 At every place in the structure of every unit, one or more choices are made. When the choice is closed, we have a system. When the choice is open, we are dealing with a lexical selection, not a grammatical one. (1961/66, 14)

649 . . . the range of possibilities in a closed choice is called technically a SYSTEM, that in an open choice a SET. As a reminder of this distinction we often talk of 'closed system' and 'open set'. (1964b, 22)

650 There are two sides to any choice situation; restriction and freedom—what we cannot choose from and what we can choose from. Each element of structure implies a choice, with these two aspects to it. (1964b, 29)

651 Wherever we can show that, at a given place in structure, the language allows for a choice among a *small fixed* set of possibilities, we have a system. Such sets of possibilities are called the TERMS in the system. (1964b, 30)

652 The choice relations are 'system', in grammar, and 'set' in lexis. (1964b, 35)

653 The choice of one feature (a given term in one system) thus becomes the environment for a choice among further features (terms in another system). (1966/76, 136)

654 . . . the grammar is based on the notion of choice. (1969/76a, 3)

655 The speaker of a language, like a person engaging in any kind of culturally determined behaviour, can be regarded as carrying out, simultaneously and successively, a number of distinct choices. (1969/76a, 3)

656 Thus the description of a linguistic item is the set of features selected in that item from the total available. (1969/76a, 4)

657 . . . the description of a sentence, clause or other item may be just a list of the choices that the speaker has made. (1969/76a, 4)

658 . . . the underlying notion in the grammar is that of choice, and this is represented through the concept of a system, which is a set of options together with a condition of entry. (1969/76a, 6)

659 It would be better, in fact, to say that we 'opt', since we are concerned not with deliberate acts of choice but with symbolic behaviour, in which the options may express our meanings only very indirectly . . . (1970b, 142)

13.2 Network

660 The network is open-ended. (1969/76a, 3)

661 I would use the term *network* for all levels, in fact: semantic network, grammatical network, phonological network. It refers simply to a representation of the potential at that level. A network is a network of options, of choices . . . (1974b, 87)

662 The network is a representation of options, more particularly of the interrelations among options. (1974b, 88)

13.3 Option

663 All syntactic options occur in the environment of other options, and the discussion of any one system is likely to require frequent reference to other systems having the same point of origin. (1967c, 215)

664 Certain options specify the presence of a particular role in the structure . . . (1967c, 215)

665 Each set of options, it was suggested, specifies its own constituent structure; in other words, each component contributes a set of possible structures whose elements, the individual functions, are combined with those of the other components to form complex elements of structure . . . (1968a, 210–11)

666 The place of each option in the grammar is specified by the location in the system network, of the system of which it is a term . . . (1969a, 253)

667 . . . one set of options may act as an environment restricting the selection or determining the interpretation of options within the other . . . (1969a, 256–7)

668 The options selected by the speaker are 'realized' as structures; and there are two aspects to a structure, the bracketing and the labelling each of which needs to be considered. (1969/76a, 4)

669 . . . options: sets of alternative meanings, which collectively account for the total meaning potential. (1971a, 55)

670 . . . all types of option, from whatever function they are derived, are meaningful. At every point the speaker is selecting among a range of possibilities that differ in meaning; and if we attempt to separate meaning from choice we are turning a valuable distinction (between linguistic functions) into an arbitrary dichotomy (between 'meaningful' and 'meaningless' choices). (1971d, 111)

671 All options are embedded in the language system: the system IS a network of options, deriving from all the various functions of language. (1971d, 111)

13.4 System

672 It may be remarked here that the polysystemic form of the description may justifiably be represented as a simplification and not a complication of the material. In language primers this poly-systematization appears when an identical form is classified under a number of different heads. (1956a, 192)

673 The distinction between closed system patterns and open set patterns in language is in fact a cline; but the theory has to treat them as two distinct types of pattern requiring different categories. (1961, 247)

674 . . . it is useful to retain 'closed system' when referring to the system as the crucial criterion for distinguishing grammar from lexis. (1961, 247)

675 A closed system is a set of terms with these characteristics:
(a) the number of terms is finite . . .
(b) each term is exclusive of all the others . . .
(c) if a new term is added to the system this changes the meaning of all the others. (1961, 247)

676 What remains to be accounted for is the occurrence of one rather than another from among a number of like events. The category set up for this purpose is the 'system'. (1961, 264)

677 . . . whenever a choice among a finite number of mutually exclusive possibilities is found to occur within a class one can recognize a system whose terms have the nature and degree of abstraction of the 'class' . . . (1961, 264–5)

678 . . . a system is a limited ('closed') set of terms in choice relation . . . (1963a, 7)

679 The closed system is . . . characteristic of grammar, the open set of lexis. (1964b, 22)

680 A property of a closed system is that its terms can be defined just as well negatively as positively . . . (1964b, 24)

681 It may be useful . . . to consider the notion of a 'systemic description' as one form of representation of a linguistic item, the assumption being that it complements but does not replace its structural description. The systemic description would be a representation of the item in terms of a set of features, each feature being in contrast with a stated set of one or more other features: being, in Firth's terms, a 'term in a system'. (1966a, 61)

682 Any pair of systems, such that a feature in one may co-occur with a feature in the other in a systemic description, may be hierarchical or simultaneous; if two systems are hierarchically ordered, features assigned to these systems are ordered likewise. (1966a, 61)

683 For any set of systems associated with a given environment it is possible to construct a system network in which each system, other than those simultaneous at the point of origin, is hierarchically ordered with respect to at least one other system. The point of origin is specified syntagmatically, so that all features are associated with a syntagmatic environment; at the same time the system network provides a paradigmatic environment for each one of the features, specifying both its contrastive status and its possibilities of combination. (1966a, 62)

684 Range of choice refers to the number of terms in a system, the number of contrastive possibilities among which a choice is made at a particular place in structure. (1966d, 180)

685 . . . a 'systemic' grammar . . . This term denotes a grammar in which the basic concept is that of the 'system' a set of features of which one and only one must be chosen if the specified conditions of entry to that system are satisfied. The grammar itself thus takes the form of a series of system networks, where each network represents the choices that are available to a given constituent type, this being the 'point of origin' of the network, and states for each choice the entry condition in terms of other choices. In other words the environment in which selection among one set of features takes place is specified in terms of other features. (1967d, 1–2)

686 We define a system as a set of options together with an entry condition, such that if the entry condition is satisfied one option from the set must be selected. (1969a, 253)

687 The name 'systemic' is not the same thing as 'systematic' . . . (1969/76a, 3)

688 It is this system that formalizes the notion of choice in language. (1969/76a, 3)

689 . . . the term /systemic/ is used because the fundamental concept in the grammar is that of the 'system'. (1969/76a, 3)

690 The system network specifies what are the possible combinations of choices that could be made; each permitted path through the network is thus the description of a class of linguistic items. (1969/76a, 4)

691 Not only does any system of linguistic features derive from some function of language, but perhaps from more than one, through which it can be related to situations of use, but in addition this fact may also determine, at least in part, the form taken by that system and its exponents in the grammar. (1970c, 361)

692 A system is an abstract representation of a paradigm . . . (1971a, 55)

693 . . . /the system network/ is a general statement of the paradigmatic relations at the stratum in question, and therefore it constitutes, at one and the same time, a description of each meaning selection and an account of its relationship to all the others . . . (1972a, 76)

694 . . . in investigating language in social contexts and settings I like to take the 'system' as the fundamental concept. (1974c, 45)

695 A system is a set of options in a stated environment; in other words, a choice, together with a condition of entry. (1974c, 45)

14
Text

14.1 Cohesion

---

696 Cohesion is a syntagmatic relation and, insofar as it is grammatical, it is partly accounted for by structure. (1964/67, 219)

697 There are certain grammatical categories whose exponents cohere with other items in the text, items to which they do not stand in a fixed structural relation or indeed necessarily in any structural relation at all. Principal among these are the anaphoric items in the nominal and adverbial group . . . (1964/67, 219)

698 We need a term to refer to a single instance of cohesion, a term for one occurrence of a pair of cohesively related items. This we shall call a TIE. (1976b, 3)

699 The concept of a tie makes it possible to analyse a text in terms of its cohesive properties, and give a systematic account of its patterns of texture. (1976b, 4)

700 The different kinds of cohesive tie . . . are: reference, substitution, ellipsis, conjunction, and lexical cohesion. (1976b, 4)

701 The concept of cohesion is a semantic one; it refers to relations of meaning that exist within the text, and that define it as a text. (1976b, 4)

702 Cohesion occurs where the INTERPRETATION of some

110

elements in the discourse is dependent on that of another. The one PRESUPPOSES the other, in the sense that it cannot be effectively decoded except by recourse to it. (1976b, 4)

703   Cohesion is part of the system of a language. The potential for cohesion lies in the systematic resources of reference, ellipsis and so on that are built into the language itself. (1976b, 5)

704   Like other semantic relations, cohesion is expressed through the stratal organization of language. (1976b, 5)

705   Cohesion is expressed partly through the grammar and partly through the vocabulary. We can refer therefore to GRAMMATICAL COHESION and LEXICAL COHESION. (1976b, 5–6)

706   . . . COHESION refers specifically to . . . non-structural textforming relations. They are . . . semantic relations, and the text is a semantic unit. (1976b, 7)

707   . . . cohesion is not, strictly speaking, a relation 'above the sentence'. It is a relation to which the sentence, or any other form of grammatical structure, is simply irrelevant. (1976b, 9)

708   . . . cohesion is a . . . general notion, and one that is above considerations of structure. (1976b, 9)

709   The concept of cohesion is set up to account for relations in discourse . . . without the implication that there is some structural unit that is above the sentence. (1976b, 10)

710   We can interpret cohesion, in practice, as the set of semantic resources for linking a SENTENCE with what has gone before. (1976b, 10)

711   . . . cohesion is not just another name for discourse structure. (1976b, 10)

712   'Cohesion' is defined as the set of possibilities that exist in the

language for making text hang together: the potential that the speaker or writer has at his disposal. (1976b, 18)

713 There remains /the/ possibility . . . that the information required for interpreting some element in the text is not to be found in the text at all, but in the situation . . . This type of reference we shall call EXOPHORA, since it takes us outside the text altogether. Exophoric reference is not cohesive, since it does not bind the two elements together into a text. (1976b, 18)

714 The concept of COHESION can . . . be usefully supplemented by that of REGISTER, since the two together effectively define a TEXT. (1976b, 23)

715 Cohesion is the set of meaning relations that is general to ALL CLASSES of text, that distinguishes text from 'non-text' and interrelates the substantive meanings of the text with each other. (1976b, 26)

716 Cohesion does not concern what a text means; it concerns how the text is constructed as a semantic edifice. (1976b, 26)

717 Cohesion is closely related to information structure, and indeed the two overlap at one point . . . (1976b, 27)

718 The general meaning of cohesion is embodied in the concept of text. (1976b, 298)

719 Cohesion expresses the continuity that exists between one part of the text and another . . . (1976b, 299)

14.2 Context of Mention

---

720 The presence of a certain form in a given unit in the syntagm may render probable the occurrence in a subsequent unit of a member of a particular class; this is in fact a form of contextual determination, but it may be stated, partially at least, in terms of only the linguistic (verbal) action in a context of situation—the source of the determination may be found to be in what might be called 'context of mention'. This requires the two-term system 'given'/'new', the given being that which has been mentioned in the preceding linguistic context. (1957, 61)

721 . . . context of mention is taken to include not only repetition of the term mentioned but also reference (for example, pronominal or synonymic). With such 'context of reference' we are well on the way towards context of situation . . . (1957, 61)

722 . . . a two-term system of context of mention: the 'given' and the 'new'. A lexical form (which may be a verb, noun or adverb), operating in a given sentence or clause, is said to be 'given' if it has been mentioned in a previous sentence or clause. The extent of operation of context of mention is not defined, though where it can be shown to operate it is to a certain degree self-defining; clearly the definition cannot be made in terms of a fixed number of clauses or sentences, but rather in terms of the relatedness of context. A sentence or clause is said to have 'related context' with a previous sentence or clause if at least one lexical form is given in the context of mention. (1959, 77)

14.3 Context of Situation

723 . . . in a spoken text, categories of given and new /are/ established in the context of situation. (1957, 61–2)

724 . . . 'situation' . . . the whole diachronic framework of events within which the text operates. (1959, 14)

725 The context is the relation of the form to non-linguistic features of the situation in which language operates, and to linguistic features other than those of the item under attention: these being together 'extratextual' features. (1961, 243–4)

726 Context is an interlevel . . . since it relates language to something that is not language; it is an interlevel because it is not with the

non-language activity itself that linguistics is concerned but with the relation of this to language form. (1961, 269)

727 . . . since context relates form to extratextual features, and is (like phonology) an interlevel, the categories of context, like those of phonology, are not determined by (still less, of course, do they determine) the categories of form; but contextual statement is required to account for all (instances of the) reflexion in form of extratextual features. (1961, 275n)

728 'Context' is the name, perhaps a rather awkward one, used by some linguists for the relation of the forms of language to non-linguistic objects and events. It thus corresponds roughly to 'meaning' in the general, non-specialized sense of the term. (1964b, 37)

729 . . . 'context of situation' . . . Essentially what this implies is that language comes to life only when functioning in some environment. (1974a, 28)

730 The 'context of situation' does not refer to all the bits and pieces of the material environment . . . It refers to those features which are relevant to the speech that is taking place. (1974a, 28)

731 Looking at how people actually use language in daily life, we find that the apparently infinite number of different possible situations represents in reality a very much smaller number of general *types* of situation . . . (1974a, 29)

732 The question is not what peculiarities of vocabulary, or grammar or pronunciation, can be directly accounted for by reference to the situation. It is *which* kinds of situational factor determine which kinds of selection in the linguistic system. The notion of register is thus a form of prediction: given that we know the situation, the social context of language use, we can predict a great deal about the language that will occur, with reasonable probability of being right. The important theoretical question then is: what do we need to know about the social context in order to make such predictions? (1974a, 33)

733 What we need to know about a context of situation in order to predict the linguistic features that are likely to be associated with it . . . /is/ the 'field of discourse', the 'mode of discourse' and the 'tenor of discourse'. (1974a, 34)

734 Being 'appropriate to the situation' is not some optional extra in language: it is an essential element in the ability to mean. (1974a, 35)

735 . . . we are interpreting the concept of 'situation' in still more abstract terms, as a semiotic structure deriving from the totality of meaning relations that constitutes the social system. This makes it possible to talk not so much about the particulars of this or that actual context of situation in which a given text is located but rather about the set of general features that characterizes a certain *situation type*. (1975c, 126)

736 . . . a situation type, a generalized social context in which text is created . . . (1975c, 130)

737 So when we stress the fact that language takes place in a context of situation, and say that a child is able to learn from what he hears because there is a systematic relation between what he hears and what is going on around him, this is not primarily because our talk is focussed on the objects and events of the external world. Much of the time it is not; and even when it is, it does not reflect their structure in any unprocessed or 'objective' way but as it is processed by the culture. The relation of talk to environment lies in the total semiotic structure of the interaction: the significant ongoing activity . . . and the social matrix within which meanings are being exchanged. (1975c, 141)

738 The significance of the exophoric potential is that, in instances where the key to the interpretation is not ready to hand, in text or situation, the hearer or reader CONSTRUCTS a context of situation in order to supply it for himself. (1976b, 18)

739 We do not, in fact, evaluate any specimen of language . . . without knowing something about its context of situation. (1976b, 20)

740 The linguistic patterns, which embody, and at the same time also impose structure on, our experience of the environment, by the same token also make it possible to identify what features of the environment are relevant to linguistic behaviour and so form part of the context of situation. (1976b, 21)

741 The more specifically we can characterize the context of situation, the more specifically we can predict the properties of a text in that situation. (1976b, 22)

742 . . . 'present in the context of situation' does not necessarily mean physically present in the interactants' field of perception; it merely means that the context of situation permits the identification to be made. (1976b, 49)

14.4 Field/Mode/Tenor

743 'Field of discourse' refers to what is going on: to the area of operation of the language activity. Under this heading, registers are classified according to the nature of the whole event of which the language activity forms a part. (1964b, 90)

744 The formal properties of any given language event will be those associated with the intersection of the appropriate field, mode and style. (1964b, 93)

745 Types of linguistic situation differ from one another, broadly speaking, in three respects: first, as regard what is actually taking place; secondly, as regards what part the language is playing; and thirdly, as regard who is taking part. These three variables, taken together, determined the range within which meanings are selected and the forms which are used for their expression, in other words, they determine the 'register'. (1974a, 32)

746 The 'field' /of discourse/ . . . refers to what the participants in the context of situation are actually engaged in doing . . . (1974a, 49)

747 . . . Tenor /of discourse/ . . . Essentially, it is the role relationships in the situation in question: who the participants in the communication group are, and in what relationship they stand to each other. (1974a, 50)

748 . . . the categories of 'field of discourse', 'mode of discourse', and 'tenor of discourse' are not themselves kinds of varieties of language. They are the backdrop, the features of the context of situation which determine the kind of language used. In other words, they determine what is often referred to as the register: that is, the types of meaning that are selected, and their expression in grammar and vocabulary. And they determine the register collectively, not piecemeal. (1974a, 50)

749 A situation type, or social context, as we understand it, is characterized by a particular semiotic structure, a complex of features which sets it apart from other situation types. This structure can then be interpreted on three dimensions: in terms of the ongoing activity (field), the role of relationships involved (tenor), and the symbolic or rhetorical channel (mode). (1975c, 130–31)

750 Field, tenor and mode are . . . the environmental determinants of text. (1975c, 131)

751 The possiblity of making such predictions /about the linguistic properties of the text that is associated with it/ appears to arise because the categories of field, tenor and mode, which we are using to describe the semiotics of the situation, are in their turn associated in a systematic way with the functional components of the semantic system. (1975c, 131)

752 Field, mode and tenor collectively define the context of situation of a text. (1976b, 22)

14.5 Register

---

753 At any particular point on the scale of delicacy the total set of registers may form a continuum, and there will certainly be a great deal that is common, linguistically, to all; but there are also linguistic differences between them—otherwise they would not be recognized as different registers. (1964a, 65)

754 And just as in dialect we eventually, by progressive refinement, reach the individual: every speaker his own idiolect, or bundle of available individual dialects: so also in register we come finally to the individual—every speaker, and writer, his own bundle of individual registers. (1964a, 65)

755 Language varies as its function varies; it differs in different situations. The name given to a variety of a language distinguished according to use is 'register'. (1964b, 87)

756 A dialect is a variety of a language distinguished according to the user . . . (1964b, 87)

757 Dialects tend to differ primarily, and always to some extent in substance. Registers, on the other hand, differ primarily in form. (1964b, 88)

758 . . . the crucial criteria of any given register are to be found in its grammar and its lexis. (1964b, 88)

759 Registers are not marginal or special varieties of language. Between them they cover the total range of our language activity. (1964b, 89)

760 It seems most useful to introduce a classification along three dimensions, each representing an aspect of the situations in which language operates and the part played by language in them. Registers, in this view, may be distinguished according to field of discourse, mode of discourse and style of discourse. (1964b, 90)

761 In the register range, the countless situations in which language activity takes place can be grouped into situation types, to which correspond the various uses of language. (1964b, 95)

762 Ultimately, register and dialect meet in the single speech event. Here we have reached the *utterance*, the smallest institutional unit of language activity. (1964b, 95)

763 Some registers are extremely restricted in purpose. They thus employ only a limited number of formal items and patterns, with the result that the language activity in these registers can accommodate little idiolectal or even dialectal variety. Such registers are known as RESTRICTED LANGUAGES. (1964b, 96)

764 The notion of register . . . It refers to the fact that the language we speak or write varies according to the type of situation . . . What the theory of register does is to attempt to uncover the general principles which govern this variation, so that we can begin to understand *what* situational factors determine *what* linguistic features. (1974a, 32)

765 The distinction between one register and another is a distinction of *what* is said as much as of *how* it is said, without any enforced separation between the two. (1974a, 35)

766 We always listen and read with expectations, and the notion of register is really a theory about these expectations, providing a way of making them explicit. (1974a, 53)

767 A register can be defined as a particular configuration of meanings that is associated with a particular situation type. (1975c, 126)

768 The register is the semantic variety of which a text is an instance. (1975c, 126)

769 Considered in terms of the notion of meaning potential, the register is the range of meaning potential that is activated by the semiotic properties of the situation. (1975c, 126)

770 The linguistic features which are typically associated with a configuration of situational features—with particular values of the field, mode and tenor—constitute a REGISTER. (1976b, 22)

771 The register is the set of meanings, the configuration of semantic patterns, that are typically drawn upon under the specified conditions, along with the words and structures that are used in the realization of these meanings. (1976b, 23)

772 The register is the set of semantic configurations that is typically associated with a particular CLASS of contexts of situation, and defines the substance of the text: WHAT IT MEANS, in the broadest sense, including the components of its meaning, social, expressive, communicative and so on as well as representational. (1976b, 26)

14.6 Speech Act

773 . . . an act of speech, regarding this as a simultaneous selection from among a large number of interrelated options. (1970b, 142)

774 Speech acts thus involve the creative and repetitive exercise of options in social and personal situations and settings. (1970b, 142)

775 Since normally every speech act serves each of the basic functions of language, the speaker is selecting among all the types of options simultaneously. Hence the various sets of structural 'roles' are mapped onto one another, so that the actual structure-forming element in language is a complex of roles, like a chord in a fugue . . . (1970b, 144)

776 A speech act is essentially a complex behaviour pattern which in most instances combines the ideational and interpersonal functions, in varying degrees of prominence. (1970b, 165)

14.7 Text

777 Any text functions in a context, from which can be abstracted certain features relevant to the descriptive analysis. (1959, 13)

778 The data to be accounted for are observed language events,

. . . any corpus of which, when used as material for linguistic description, is a 'text'. (1961, 243)

779 The linguist operates with *language* and *text*, the latter referring to all linguistic material, spoken or written, which we observe in order to study language. The linguist's object of study is the language and his object of observation is the text: he describes language and relates it to the situations in which it is operating. (1961/66, 18)

780 The linguistic study of literature is textual description, and it is no different from any other textual description; it is not a new branch or a new level or a new kind of linguistics but the application of existing theories and methods. (1964a, 64)

781 For our purposes it is important that as much as possible of ordinary speech should be shown to be—that is, described as—nondeviant . . . But there are deviant structures, and it is important to specify in what ways they are deviant. (1964c, 194)

782 A text is meaningful not only in virtue of what it is but also in virtue of what it might have been. (1964/67, 217)

783 . . . a linguistic analysis will relate the text to the language as a whole. (1964/67, 217)

784 The basic unit of language in use is not a word or a sentence but a 'text' . . . (1970b, 160)

785 A *text* is an operational unit of language, as a sentence is a syntactic unit . . . It is the text and not some super-sentence that is the relevant unit for stylistic studies; this is a functional-semantic concept and is not definable by size. And therefore the 'textual' function is not limited to the establishment of relations between sentences; it is concerned just as much with the internal organization of the sentence, with its meaning as a message both in itself and in relation to the context. (1971d, 107)

786 . . . language will be recognized as playing some role only if it is acceptable as text. (1974c, 48)

787   . . . 'text' is language in use. (1974c, 48)

788   The speaker's command of his language includes an awareness of the difference between text and non-text—lists of words, or random sets of sentences. (1974c, 48)

789   Normally /the speaker/ will assume that what he hears or reads is text, and he will go to great lengths to justify his assumption and ensure that communication is taking place. This assumption is a functional one; it rests not so much on recognizing words and structures as on recognizing the role that language is playing in the situation. (1974c, 48)

790   . . . we see the text as actualized potential; it is the actual seen against the background of the potential. (1974b, 86)

791   To me the concept of text is to be defined by level of abstraction, not by size. In other words, *text is to semantics* what sentence is to grammar. A sentence is to be defined as a fundamental unit of grammar, and we don't define the sentence as a kind of super-phoneme. Now, in the same way, the text is to be defined as a fundamental unit of semantics, and we don't define it as a kind of supersentence. (1974b, 101)

792   . . . text is meaning. A text is a semantic unit, realized as (encoded in) lexicogrammatical units which are further realized as (recoded in) phonological or orthographic units. (1975c, 123)

793   What are the essential properties of text? It is meaning, and it is choice. (1975c, 123)

794   Any instance of language that is operational, as distinct from citational (like sentences in a grammar book, or words listed in a dictionary), is text. (1975c, 123)

795   Text is 'what is meant'—presupposing a background of what might have been meant but was not. (1975c, 124)

796   The word TEXT is used in linguistics to refer to any passage, spoken or written, of whatever length, that does form a unified whole. (1976b, 1)

797 A text is best regarded as a SEMANTIC unit: a unit not of form but of meaning. (1976b, 2)

798 A text does not CONSIST of sentences; it is REALIZED BY, or encoded in, sentences. (1976b, 2)

799 A text . . . is not a structural unit . . . (1976b, 6)

800 In general, any unit which is structured hangs together so as to form text. All grammatical units . . . are internally 'cohesive' simply because they are structured. The same applies to the phonological units . . . (1976b, 7)

801 Under normal circumstances, of course, we do not find ourselves faced with 'non-text', which is 'non-sense' of a rather esoteric kind. (1976b, 23)

802 A text is a passage of discourse which is coherent in these two regards: it is coherent with respect to the context of situation, and therefore consistent in register; and it is coherent with respect to itself, and therefore cohesive. (1976b, 23)

803 /A text/ is to semantic structure what the sentence is to lexicogrammatical structure and the syllable to phonological structure. (1976b, 25)

804 A text, then, can be thought of as the basic unit of meaning in language. (1976b, 25)

805 /A text/ is a unit of situational-semantic organization: a continuum of meaning-in-context, constructed around the semantic relation of cohesion. (1976b, 25)

806 Being present in the text is, as it were, a special case of being present in the situation. (1976b, 32)

807 Language does not function in isolation; it functions as TEXT, in actual situations of use. (1976b, 142)

808 . . . the text—the linguistic component of the communication process . . . (1976b, 267)

14.8 Texture

---

809 The concept of TEXTURE is entirely appropriate to express the property of 'being a text'. A text has texture, and this is what distinguishes it from something that is not a text. It derives this texture from the fact that it functions as a unity with respect to its environment. (1976b, 2)

810 Texture is a matter of degree. (1976b, 23)

811 . . . texture involves more than the presence of semantic relations of the kind we refer to as cohesive . . . It involves also some degree of coherence in the actual meanings expressed: not only, or even mainly, in the CONTENT, but in the TOTAL selection from the semantic resources of the language, including the various interpersonal (social–expressive–conative) components—the moods, modalities, intensities, and other forms of the speaker's intrusion into the speech situation. (1976b, 23)

812 Texture results from the combination of semantic configurations of two kinds: those of register, and those of cohesion. (1976b, 26)

813 The main components of texture within the sentence in English are the theme systems and the information systems. (1976b, 325)

15
Theory & Description

814 The scheme of categories is put forward as one possible scheme devised in order to account for all the facts in as economical a way as possible. It is not offered as the only possible scheme; the description may vary according to the purpose envisaged by the linguist and, even granted an identity of purpose, there will still remain a number of alternative possibilities in the statement. (1956a, 177)

815 . . . the need for a *general* theory of description, as opposed to a *universal* scheme of descriptive categories, has long been apparent if often unformulated, in the description of all languages. (1957, 54)

816 If we consider general linguistics to be the body of theory which guides and controls the procedures of the various branches of linguistic science, then any linguistic study, historical or descriptive, particular or comparative, draws on and contributes to the principles of general linguistics. (1957, 55)

817 Any of these types of study /historical, descriptive, particular and comparative/ may be undertaken with the use of formal linguistic methods: that is, by the methods of what is sometimes called 'structural linguistics'. (If such a term is to be used, it should perhaps be taken to refer neither to a branch nor to a particular school of linguistics but to that body of general linguistic theory which controls the application of formal linguistic techniques.) (1957, 55)

818 A third horizontal axis /to particular and comparative/ in terms of the scope of the material might be the 'universal'; the question is whether this is at present . . . 'on the agenda', since what is formal when particular or comparative tends to become imaginative when universal. (1957, 56)

819 While perhaps modern general linguistics would recognize the establishment of categories within the language under description itself as the basis of a particular description, reference to the forms of another language, including the language of description, may be made without infringing the requirements of formal analysis. (1957, 62)

820 Since language is used to describe language, if in a formal descriptive grammar it is desired to exclude from consideration as far as possible all forms that do not belong to the l.u.d., the nearest approach is that . . . where the aim is achieved through the creation of a metalanguage whose terms, whatever the context of their previous usage, are to be taken as defined only with reference to the text under description. All identification of categories either comparative or universal is thereby excluded. (1957, 62)

821 The procedures of descriptive grammar are deduced from the principles of linguistic science in accordance with the place of descriptive analysis in the framework of general linguistics. (1959, 7)

822 The descriptive technique is applicable to all texts, of any extent, spoken or written; the description requires only that the text shall be circumscribed so that the statements refer to the language of the text and are made as valid only for that text. (1959, 8)

823 While for the purpose of descriptive grammar a text is circumscribed and statements are made as valid only for that text, it is true nevertheless that with a written text one can set up certain criteria for placing it in the context of a corpus of written texts which together constitute one 'language' (état de langue); statements made as valid for one text in the corpus may then be taken unless disproved to apply to the others. Such a corpus requires a unity, whose limits cannot be generalized, of time, place, language and style. (1959, 18)

824 There are . . . as it were two poles from which the language which is the medium of the description impinges upon the language under description. In the systematic statement of grammatical categories the terminology of the description is as it were collocated afresh: it becomes itself a restricted lexical system in the 'metalanguage' of description. At the opposite pole lies the translation of the text in the language of description. The difficulty lies in the search for points of contact between the language of the text and intermediate regions of the language of description. (1959, 69)

825 There have been in the main two approaches to description in modern linguistics: the 'textual' and the non-textual or, for want of a better word, 'exemplificatory'. More recently a third has been added, primarily in grammar but lately also in phonology, the 'generative' (strictly 'transformational-generative', since generation does not presuppose transformation). Some linguists have gone so far as to suggest that transformative generation should replace other types of description as a linguistic method of making statements about language. Others, myself included, feel that all three approaches have a fundamental place in linguistics; that they do different things, and that the third is a valuable supplement to the first two. (1961, 241)

826 . . . any theory-based grammar, transformational or not, can be stated in generative terms. (1961, 241n)

827 One part of General Linguistics theory is a theory of how language works. It is from this that the methods of Descriptive Linguistics are derived. (1961, 242)

828 Description consists in relating the text to the categories of the theory. (1961, 243)

829 . . . General Linguistic theory must here provide both a theory of

grammar and a theory of lexis, and also a means of relating the two. (1961, 247)

830 In this view of linguistic description is . . . a body of method derived from a theory, and *not* a set of procedures. (1961, 249)

831 A theory . . . provides a means for evaluating descriptions without reference to the order in which the facts are accounted for. (1961, 249)

832 The best description is . . . that which, comprehensiveness presupposed, is maximally grammatical: that is, makes maximum use of the theory to account for a maximum amount of the data. Simplicity has then to be invoked only when it is necessary to decide between fewer systems with more terms and more systems with fewer terms: and since both information theory and linguistic intuition favour the latter even this preference might be built in to the theory. (1961, 249)

833 . . . is it true that 'it is unreasonable to demand of linguistic theory that it provide anything more than a practical evaluation procedure for grammars'? (Chomsky, *Syntactic Structures*) This it must do. But it can be asked to do more: to provide a framework of logically interrelated categories (so that it can be evaluated as a theory, and compared with other theories) from which can be derived methods of description, whether textual, exemplificatory, or transformative-generative, which show us something of how language works. (1961, 291–2)

834 . . . 'general linguistics' . . . the whole body of theory, linguistic and phonetic, that lies behind the study of language. (1961/66, 2)

835 'General linguistics' implies a general theory of language, and this in turn implies that we can identify the properties that are common to all languages and distinguish these from the features that are specific to a given language. (1961/66, 2)

836 The basic principle of description is to analyse the language according to its various kinds of patterning: to break it down into what we call 'levels'. (1961/66, 3)

837 Observation, generalization, theory, presentation: this, one might perhaps say, is the scientific method of description. The facts of language are such that we must proceed by a set of abstractions at several levels at once, all constantly interrelated but each level having its own categories. These categories enable us to arrange systematically the mass of events constituting a language. (1961/66, 5)

838 It should be stressed that linguistic descriptions are not, so to speak, monovalent. A description is not simply 'right' or 'wrong' in itself (it may be wrong, of course, if it does not conform to the facts); it is better thought of as more useful or less . . . The aim is to find the simplest description that will account for all the facts, and one often has to have described a considerable area of the language before being able to judge which of two possibilities is the simpler. (1961/66, 9)

839 When we undertake a comparative description of two languages, we have as it were two kinds of evidence at our disposal. The first is translation equivalence; the second is formal comparison. (1961/66, 32)

840 In the comparison of languages we may take advantage of the fact that . . . there are always several different ways of describing the same linguistic phenomenon; it is thus possible to adapt the description of one language to that of another. The aim of this 'transfer comparison' is to draw attention to the resemblances between the two languages. (1961/66, 39)

841 We must admit . . . that general linguistics has sometimes given the impression of dehydrating language; the fault perhaps lies with out own interpretation of those who sought, understandably, to free themselves from the tyranny of mentalism and of ideas, from the demand that 'the ideas behind' language, rather than language itself, should be described, and thus attempted to exclude considerations of meaning. (1961/66, 40)

842 A description of a language, if it is to be of practical use, must be based on a general theory; a theory of language if it is to remain in

touch with reality, must be tested in the description of languages. There is no cleavage between the pure and the applied in linguistics; on the contrary, each flourishes only where the other is also flourishing. (1961/66, 41)

843 Within descriptive linguistics, one kind of description is textual: the linguist describes a text, written or spoken; this contrasts with exemplificatory description, which represents the categories of the language and illustrates them, or, if formalized, generates a set of described sentences and derives others from them. (1964a, 64)

844 To study language scientifically means to construct a unified theory of how language works, and to derive from it certain exact methods for describing languages. The theory is not of course conjured out of the air: it has its origins in countless observations of language events. Once a theory has been constructed its relation to the observations, which we refer to as 'abstractions' (to be understood as a relation, not as a process), may take various forms; in one way or another the theory exercises control over the statements made within its range of operation. (1964b, 5)

845 If we say that linguistics is partly a 'logical' study, this is not to be taken to imply that there is any relation between logic and *language*, that propositional or predicate logic can be used to explain the relations between linguistic items . . . What we do imply is a relation between logic and *linguistics*: that a symbolic or 'scientific logic' may be considered to underlie the *theoretical* validity of the categories used to describe language, and the consistency of their relations to each other within the total framework of categories. (1964b, 13)

846 It is not true that only one model can represent the nature of language; language is much too complex for any one model to highlight all its different aspects equally clearly. (1964b, 18)

847 . . . as soon as a single statement is made about the grammar of a language, a theory is implied. (1964b, 32)

848 For the description of a language to be of the greatest use, it must account for contextual as well as formal patterns. (1964b, 40)

849 . . . the branch of linguistics which deals, to put it in the most general terms, with the relation between a language and the people who use it. This includes the study of language communities, singly and in contact, of varieties of language and of attitudes to language. The various special subjects involved here are grouped together under the name of 'institutional linguistics'. (1964b, 75)

850 Languages in contact, dialects and registers are three of the major topics of institutional linguistics. The fourth . . . is the observation of the attitudes of members of a language community towards their language and its varieties. (1964b, 98)

851 The theories and methods for the comparison of languages, including theory of translation, belong to the branch of the subject known as 'Comparative Linguistics'. (1964b, 112)

852 Each language is a complex of a large number of patterns, at different levels and at different degrees of delicacy: a 'system of systems', in one well-known formulation. There can be no single, general statement accounting for all of these, and therefore no overall comparative statement accounting for the difference between two languages. (1964b, 113)

853 Every comparative statement presupposes three steps: first, the separate description of the relevant features of each language: second, the establishment of comparability; third, the comparison itself. (1964b, 113–14)

854 There is a special method for comparing the grammar of languages which differs somewhat from ordinary comparative descriptive; this ıs known as 'transfer comparison'. Comparison in the normal way brings together two languages which have been separately and independently described, with the categories appropriate to each; such comparison is therefore neutral, as it were, and gives equal weight to the languages concerned. In transfer comparison, on the other hand, one starts from the description of one language and then describes the second language in terms of the categories set up for the first. (1964b, 120)

855 If a language, or a text, is described with the sole aim of finding out more about language, or about that particular language, this is a use of linguistic theory but it is not an application of linguistics. Applied linguistics starts when a description is specifically made, or an existing description used, for a further purpose which lies outside the linguistic science. (1964b, 138)

856 Theories can always be replaced by better theories, new facts elicited and new syntheses made. The applications themselves are an important source of feedback: a theory is constantly re-examined in the light of ideas suggested in the course of its application. If a theory is allowed to stand still, it soon ceases to be useful. (1964b, 139)

857 All linguistics is structural, in the sense that a description must account for the internal patterns of language, and this can only be achieved if the criteria are drawn from within and not from outside language. At the same time all statements about language are statements of meaning, and the task of the linguist is to work out, from observations of language in action, theories of how language works which will enable him best to make such statements. (1964b, 151)

858 . . . I would defend the view that different co-existing models in linguistics may best be regarded as appropriate to different aims, rather than as competing contenders for the same goal. (1964c, 191)

859 In assessing the value of a description, it is reasonable to ask whether it has proved useful for the purpose for which it is intended; and such purposes may be external as well as internal to linguistics. (1964c, 191)

860 The nature of a grammatical description, in fact, is determined as a whole by the properties of the model in which it has status, as well as being conditioned by the goals that lie behind the model. (1964c, 193)

861 In interlinguistic classification . . . the aim is to classify not the items within a language but the languages themselves. (1966d, 165)

862 Interlinguistic classification is an essential part of the description of any language; it is here that, out of the progression of events that constitute a language, we abstract units—word, syllable and so on—and classes of these units, such as 'dependent clause', 'verb (word)' and 'long syllable'. (1966d, 165)

863 If languages are to be compared, they must be described in the same terms according to a general framework for the description of language, or general linguistic theory. (1966d, 174)

864 . . . /linguistics/ is . . . a unified field, with its own range of tasks and objectives, and we should perhaps be wary of any cleavage between for example a linguistics that looks to psychology as its nearest relative and one which looks to sociology and social anthropology. The psychologist, concerned primarily with human constraints, or at least not culturally determined variables, may seek to make all languages look alike; the sociologist, concerned with the diversity of human cultures, is predisposed for languages to look different. Neither is wrong; all languages are alike and all languages are different. But this is not a simple dichotomy. We cannot simply say that all languages are alike underneath and different on the surface, and the work of Whorf is a useful reminder here. A grammar is not thereby less perspicuous because it embodies an empirical attitude towards the concrete universals of description. (1967f, 27–8)

865 Linguistics is not as a rule concerned with the description of particular speech events on individual occasions . . . It is concerned rather with the description of speech acts, or texts, since only through the study of language in use are all the functions of language, and therefore all components of meaning, brought into focus. (1970b, 145)

866 There is a sense in which /linguistics/ is autonomous, and has to be if it is to be relevant to other fields of study: the particulars of language are explained by reference to a general account of language, not by being related piecemeal to social or other non-linguistic phenomena. But this 'autonomy' is conditional and temporary; in the last analysis, we cannot insulate the subject within its own boundaries, and when we come to decide what features in language are to be ignored as unsystematic we are bound to invoke considerations from outside language itself. (1971a, 53)

867 . . . a linguistic description is a statement of what the speaker can mean . . . (1972a, 79)

868 Any study of language involves some attention to other disciplines; one cannot draw a boundary round the subject and insulate it from others. (1974a, 6–7)

869 The exploration of language cannot be neatly classified as natural science, social science, humanity or fine art: it takes something from each of these world views. (1974a, 66)

870 It seems to me that we have to recognize different purposes for which language may be studied. An autonomous linguistics is the study of language for the sake of understanding the linguistic system. An instrumental linguistics is the study of language for understanding something else—the social system, for example. (1974b, 83)

871 . . . there are two different issues involved when you talk about autonomy. One is: 'To what extent *is* the subject self-sufficient?' My answer is: 'It isn't.' (But then what subject is?) The second is: 'To what extent *are we studying* language for the purpose of throwing light on language or for the purpose of throwing light on something else?' This is a question of goals; it is the question why you are doing it. In this sense the two perspectives are just complementary. (1974b, 83)

872 I am not really interested in the boundaries between disciplines;

but if you pressed me for one specific answer, I would have to say that for me linguistics is a branch of sociology. Language is part of the social system, and there is no need to interpose a psychological level of interpretation. (1974b, 85)

873 For any system one may look either at its internal structure /synchronic/ or at the process by which it evolved and reached that structure /diachronic/. But I personally am very much in sympathy with the trend which puts these two perspectives closely together, in the sense that either can be used to illuminate the other. (1974b, 100)

Alphabetical Listing of Terms